The Astrologers and their Creed

Christopher McIntosh

The Astrologers and their Creed
an historical outline

WITH A FOREWORD BY AGEHANANDA BHARATI

FREDERICK A. PRAEGER, *Publishers*

New York · Washington

BOOKS THAT MATTER

Published in the United States of America in 1969
by Frederick A. Praeger, Inc., Publishers
111 Fourth Avenue, New York, N.Y. 10003

© 1969, in London, England, by Christopher McIntosh

Library of Congress Catalog Card Number: 73–93303

Printed in Great Britain

To my wife Robina and to my parents

Contents

Illustrations

Figures in the text

The illustration on the binding is from the *Stella Nova* of
Johannes Kepler, Royal Astronomical Society and *Ronan
Picture Library*.

Acknowledgements

Among the many people who have helped me with this book, I would like to give my special thanks to the following: my wife, for sharing much of the labour in producing the manuscript; Professor Agehananda Bharati, for writing the foreword and for his advice on certain parts of the text; Mr. Ellic Howe, for providing me with much material from his own researches into the recent history of astrology; and Dr. Daniel Brostoff of the editorial staff of Hutchinson & Co., for his kind interest and help throughout all stages of the book's production.

I would also like to thank the following publishers for permission to quote from books published by them: The American Philosophical Society; Cambridge University Press; Columbia University Press; W. Foulsham & Co.; The Hamlyn Publishing Group; William Kimber & Co.; Vittorio Klostermann; Luzac & Co.; Macmillan & Co., Trinity College, Cambridge and Mr. M. B. Yeats; Ninth House Publishing Co.; Oxford University Press; Penguin Books; Editions Planète; Princeton University Press; Routledge and Kegan Paul; Schocken Books Inc.; Secker and Warburg; Stanford University Press; Theosophical Publishing House; Vincent Stuart and John M. Watkins; Yale University Press.

Foreword

Astrology has been a *bête noire* to many a shepherd: the doctors
of the great religions either rejected it or they frowned upon
it, with very few exceptions—and their more zealous followers
persecuted the practitioners; ancient and medieval emperors
and kings were fascinated by it, but they feared the astrologer
who would read the stars against them; modern political and
religious charismatics officially scoff at the art and its per-
formers—and yet (the author's statement notwithstanding)
quite a few of them have clandestine recourse to it—I am
thinking of Hitler and Hess, who had their own court astrologers in secret, even when they persecuted all other practitioners.
Modern scientists and scholars, in the Western world at least,
deny astrology even a theoretical lease on life: but there are
notable exceptions. Some of my own anthropological and
orientalist colleagues swear by it, refusing to enlist the orthodox
scientific argument of the *non-sequitur* type when talking about
astrology. But the professors at the academies of the Western
world do not even get annoyed at people who want to establish
astrology as a science, much as they no longer get annoyed at
people who want to sell a *perpetuum mobile*. I am afraid that
nothing of what Mr. McIntosh has to say in this fascinating
volume is likely to sway the diehard scientists and scholars
around the Atlantic.

The situation is quite different in the East. In all Asian countries I believe, but in India, Pakistan, Ceylon, and many other Southern Asian areas I know that all people, including professional scientists, not only believe in astrology's workings very much like the people the author writes about, but they seek the astrologer's counsel for such routine things as the marriages of their children, inceptive actions, and more general advice. The most sophisticated and the most westernised in India today take the astrologer for granted, and the apologetic vis-à-vis the critical West runs somewhat like 'we don't really believe in it, but our elders do and we do not want to hurt them'. Be that as it may, if we were to tabulate the learned of the earth, in a single continuum, without grouping them by country and nation, the believers and the users of astrology would outnumber the opponents—which, objectively, does not really mean much for or against it, since it is well known that all Frenchmen *may* be wrong, including the General.

Christopher McIntosh has tried to do several things, and he has done them well: in the first place, he has given us a fine historical account of astrology from its Babylonian beginnings to our contemporary scene; there may be more erudite accounts, and more elaborate ones, but they would be much longer and much less accessible; or else they are written by believers, converts, and other enthusiasts. It is not really relevant whether the author is a believer—he writes with sympathy and empathy, and I do not think that anyone, believer or opponent, could have produced a better account unless he set out to write a work of pure footnoted scholarship, one of those impressive bibliographies with a commentary which stand for classical historical erudition—but such was not the purpose of this author. This is an eminently readable book, and one that disproves the *obiter dictum* of my illustrious colleague Professor Nicolai Nicolayevitch Poppe, the world's foremost Mongolist, who said in a faculty meeting (in a heavy Russo-German accent) 'a good book is a boring book—a bad book is an interesting book'.

Let me conclude my say with a statement of my own faith: I do not believe in astrology in any sense. I have seen amazingly correct predictions made about persons, fates, and events, by astrologers, especially in India; but they haven't changed my mind a bit, simply because statistics go against their case—astrologers and their votaries tend to ignore or forget the predominant misfirings over the few bull's-eyes, because the latter are so impressive. But more than the lack of empirical corroboration, it is the logical and the ethical aspect of it that bars me from even trying to enter the circle of the adepts: logically, there can be no correlation between the stars and people, because no chain of human events can even theoretically be shown to follow the motions of bodies in space—and like all metaphysical utterances, astrological statements cannot be verified *or* falsified—for just like God's goodness or the pervasiveness of an Absolute Power, the astrological theses cannot answer the one question which any set of statements must pass before it can make the claim to be scientific: what sort of events would the astrologer consider as *refuting* his art? The answer is 'none'—for whatever happens, or does not happen, is precisely a proof to him. Astrology, like all other metaphysics, does not make any concession for those who are not ready to accept anything and everything as proof.

On the ethical side, I confess that I tend to think the assumptions of astrology to be morally unacceptable: for if our life is determined—be that *in toto* or *in parte*—then moral responsibility is abridged for the individual. McIntosh quotes many answers to this charge, preferred as it was throughout the ages. But as an irreparable indeterminist, I will not accept moral determinism from outside, however segmentary. I have studied this script with zest, amazement and some amusement; it does not change my views—but it does make me more lenient, and perchance more interested, in people who (McIntosh's quote from the literature which he has purveyed) 'waste their time studying how others have wasted their time'. Thus, believers will enjoy this work of love, as grist to their mills—and non-believers, as grist to theirs. . . .

AGEHANANDA BHARATI
Professor of Anthropology
Syracuse University, New York

Preface

'Consider the aspects of the disastrous influenza schemozzle.'
The main words of that unlikely sentence have an interesting
thing in common. They are all derived from astrology.
Consider and disaster come from two different Latin words
meaning star; aspect was originally used exclusively to mean
the angle between two planets in a person's horoscope;
influenza is an Italian word meaning influence, in this case the
influence of the stars; and schemozzle comes from two Yiddish
words, *schlimm* and *Mazzal*, which together mean 'bad heaven'
or 'evil constellation'. These words and many more of astrological origin have become so familiar that few people, apart
from etymologists, ever stop to wonder where they came from
or how they became so deeply entrenched in our language.
Yet their presence is an indication of the firm background of
belief in astrology from which they emerged.

Today most people regard astrology as, at best, a harmless
indulgence enjoyed by the readers of the horoscope pages of
national newspapers, and, at worst, an irritating remnant of
medieval superstition. Yet an increasing minority of serious-
minded people are following Carl Jung's example in regarding
it as a subject worthy of deeper consideration. This is not
because astrology has made itself scientifically respectable; it is
because science itself is beginning to lose its respectability.

More and more people are becoming conscious of the fact that, while man's environment has been made more intelligible by science, man himself has become a deeper mystery than ever. It is becoming increasingly apparent that, where man is concerned, our scientific and rational way of looking at things is in many respects less revealing and less helpful than the more symbolic ways employed by the Babylonians, the ancient Egyptians, the Chinese, the Greeks, and the other great civilisations of the past. Astrology is one aspect of this symbolic conception of the world, and my purpose is to make possible a clearer reappraisal of it by tracing its development from its earliest origins and examining the various forms in which it has been practised at different times and in different countries.

Astrology comes into an odd category among human pursuits. There are certain activities, like eating, that are practised wherever mankind exists. There are certain others, like smoking, that are the inventions of particular societies and then spread throughout the world. Astrology lies between the two, being an art that has been practised by almost every civilisation throughout the world and yet has developed along lines determined by the particular time, place, and historical setting in which it arose. The river of astrology has many tributaries, but all of them join up with a mainstream whose source is in ancient Babylon. To follow this river through history is to take an interesting route, touching on religion, politics, magic, art, literature and even music. I hope the reader will pardon me for turning aside occasionally to explore a tantalising branch of the stream.

1969   C.A.M.

Chapter 1   The origins of astrology

Early star lore

The heavenly bodies have long been a rich source of myth and an inexhaustible subject for speculation. What is the purpose of the Sun, Moon and stars? What are they made of? Where did they come from? These are the sort of questions that man has asked himself ever since it first occurred to him to turn his face towards the sky; and because the sky is an inescapable part of the environment of all men, these questions have been asked in all communities throughout the world.

Myths woven around the celestial bodies are part of the folklore of all nations and enter into all the great religions of the world. Any study of the star cults and astrological systems of the more highly developed civilisations must therefore begin with an examination of the fundamental reverence for the heavens which is the common heritage of all societies.

The Sun is the most obvious object of veneration to primitive peoples. It takes no great sophistication to perceive that the Sun is responsible for seasonal changes and that all life on Earth is dependent on its heat. What could be more natural than to regard this beneficent body as a god? And from the deification of the Sun it is a short step to the deification of the Moon and stars.

One of the facts most striking to the stargazer must have been the permanent, immortal character of the heavenly bodies; and many myths grew up explaining this immortality. An example is the story told among the Utopos of the Congo. One day, it is said, God summoned to him the inhabitants of the Moon and of the Earth. The former answered the call immediately and God said to the Moon: 'As a reward for coming at my summons, you shall not die, except for two days each month, and then only to rest, after which you will appear brighter than ever.' But when the Earth's inhabitants arrived much later, God was angry at their tardiness and said to them: 'You did not come at my summons, and to punish you, you shall die one day, and never live again except to come to me.'[1]

Another source of myth was the question of the origin of the heavenly bodies. Among certain peoples of the Pacific the Sun and Moon are regarded as being children of a deity or of the first men. In the Celebes the Sun, Moon and stars are thought to have been formed from the body of a heavenly girl. In the mythology of the people of Nias the Sun and Moon were formed from the eyes of an armless and legless being from whose heart sprang the tree with the buds which were the origin of men and gods.

In certain other islands of the Pacific the Sun and Moon are regarded as beings who have passed from the earth to the sky. In the Admiralty islands, for example, there is a story that the first couple to inhabit the earth made mushrooms and threw them into the sky. The one thrown by the man became the Moon. The other, thrown by the woman, became the Sun. In the New Hebrides the Sun and Moon are thought of as a husband and wife who lived on earth for a time and then climbed into the sky.

Similar myths are woven around the stars. In the Marquesas, for example, large stars are believed to be the children of the Sun and Moon who have multiplied among themselves. In certain Australian aborigine tribes there is a belief that alpha

[1] Max Fauconnet, *Mythology of Black Africa, Larousse Encyclopedia of Mythology.*

and beta Centauri are two brothers who ascended into heaven after achieving various heroic deeds.[1]

Through such myths as these the heavenly bodies are shown to be a universal preoccupation exercising almost as strong an influence on mythology as the other inescapable facts of existence such as birth and death. But it is not only among primitive peoples that a reverence for the stars is to be found. As civilised communities develop there emerges a need for an accurate measurement of time. And as time is measured from the movements of the heavenly bodies, the study of astronomy is a prerequisite for the formation of a calendar. All civilisations which had a calendar also had, to varying degrees of sophistication, a system of astronomy.

It is now known, for example, that the many megalithic sites in Britain were constructed, some as early as 2000 BC, for the purpose of marking solstices and other important astronomical events so that an accurate calendar could be kept. One authority on the subject writes, of the men who built them: 'We need not be surprised that their calendar was a highly developed arrangement involving an exact knowledge of the length of the solar year or that they had set up many stations for observing the eighteen-year cycle of the revolution of the lunar nodes.'[2]

Although we do not know what religious significance the ancient Britons attributed to the stars, it is very likely that they regarded them with more than a scientific interest. Historical records of a much later period show that the Druids worshipped the Moon and stars as destinations of departed souls. They believed that the soul passed from one heavenly body to another as it experienced successively more exalted states of existence. So convinced were they of the existence of a future life in the stars that they lent money to one another on the understanding that it would be repaid in the other world.[3]

[1] G-H. Luquet, *Mythology of Oceania, Larousse Encyclopedia of Mythology.*
[2] A. Thom, *Megalithic Sites in Britain.*
[3] Flammarion, *History of the Heavens.* Tr. J. F. Blake.

Babylonian astrology

The mainstream of astrology has its source in an area which was also the source of Western civilisation—the fertile crescent of the Middle East. It was here that man first laid down his hunting weapons, abandoned the nomadic life, and settled down with plough and scythe to develop an agricultural society. With agriculture came more leisure and more disciplined government, and with these came organised religion with its temples and priests.

It was the priests of the kingdom of Babylonia ~~who~~ made the discovery which set the pattern for the development of ~~astronomy and of~~ the zodiacal system of astrology that we know today. For many generations they had been meticulously observing and recording the movements of the heavenly bodies. Finally they had, by careful calculation, discovered that there were, besides the Sun and Moon, five other visible planets which moved in established courses through the sky. These were the planets that we now call Mercury, Venus, Mars, Jupiter and Saturn.

The discovery which these priest-astronomers made was a remarkable one, considering how crude ~~were~~ the instruments ~~with which they worked~~. They had no telescopes, ~~nor any of~~ the complicated apparatus which astronomers use today. But they did ~~have~~ one big advantage. The area, next to the Persian Gulf, on which their kingdom ~~lay~~, was ~~blessed with~~ extremely clear skies. In order to make full use of this advantage they built towers on flat areas of country and from these were able to scan the entire horizon.

These priests lived highly secluded lives in monasteries usually adjacent to the towers. Every day they observed the movements of the heavenly spheres ~~and noted down any corresponding earthly phenomena from flood to rebellions~~. Very early on they had come to the conclusion that the laws which governed the movements of the stars and planets also governed events on Earth. The seasons changed with the movements of the Sun, therefore, they argued, the other heavenly bodies must surely ~~exercise~~ a similar influence. The reports which they made were signed by the observer *were* and presented to the king who preserved them in the royal library. They were later gathered together in a collection of writings known as the *Enuma Anu Ellil* which was preserved by the Assyrians after their conquest of Babylon.

In the early stages of the Babylonian religion the stars and planets were regarded as being actual gods. Later, however, as the religion became more sophisticated, the two ideas were separated and the belief developed that the god ruled the corresponding planet.

Gradually, a highly complex system was built up in which each planet had a particular set of properties ascribed to it. This system was developed partly through the reports of the priests and partly through the natural characteristics of the planets. Mars, for example, was seen to be red in colour and was therefore identified with the god Nergal, the fiery god of war and destruction. Venus was most prominent in the morning, giving birth, as it were, to the day. She therefore became the planet associated with the female qualities of love and gentleness as well as with the function of procreation.

The Babylonians were aware of the distinction between stars and planets. To them the stars formed a background against which the planets moved. The background itself moved in a yearly cycle, but the patterns on it never changed. The planets, by contrast, were not fixed. Each one took a different length of time to complete its cycle and therefore the combination of planetary positions never repeated itself.

Besides the planets, the other great discovery that the Babylonians made was that of the zodiac. It would help us to understand how this concept was evolved if we stepped back for a moment and imagined ourselves in the position of the Babylonians. Let us imagine that we are conscious of the passage of time and aware that this consciousness of time is related in some way to the movements of the heavenly bodies. How, in these circumstances, would we set about establishing a formal way of recording the passage of time?

The first thing a community in this position would notice would be the alternation of day and night. Next, they would observe the solar year with its changing seasons. The members of the community would be aware that there was a high point of summer and a low point of winter, and also that there was a half-way point between winter and summer and between summer and winter. These points are what we would now call the solstices and the equinoxes. The diagram below explains these terms more clearly. The sphere is the Earth and the horizontal circle round it represents the equator (imagining

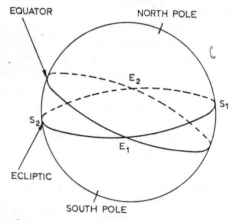

The ecliptic and equatorial co-ordinates

that the Earth's axis is vertical). The tilted circle represents the *ecliptic*, that is the path that the Sun appears to trace around the Earth during the course of a year. The equinoxes are the points where the ecliptic crosses the equator, once in the spring and once in the autumn. These are marked as E_1 and E_2 (respectively). The solstices are the highest points of summer and winter and are shown as S_1 and S_2. If one lived in the northern hemisphere S_1 would be the summer solstice and S_2 the winter one, and vice-versa for the southern hemisphere.

The next thing that a simple community would become aware of would be the fact that there are approximately twelve lunar cycles in the solar year. In dividing up the year, it would be natural, therefore, to divide it into twelve parts.

The next question is: how would one characterise these twelve parts? This is where the stars would come in. At first the Babylonians marked the stages of the year by identifying them with particular stars that rose at different seasons. This proved to be unsatisfactory since the stars were unpredictable in the times at which they were visible. They then hit on the method of identifying the twelve months with twelve different constellations along the ecliptic. It was this system which developed into that of the zodiacal signs.

The way in which the signs got their names is more complex than is usually thought. The most popular theory pictures a Babylonian shepherd gazing up at the night sky and seeing in the stars the shapes of animals and men—here, a ram, there, a bull and so on. From these shapes, it is supposed, developed the signs of the zodiac and the qualities attributed to them.

This theory immediately becomes doubtful when we look at the shapes of the constellations, most of which do not remotely resemble the objects whose names they bear. For example, how could the amorphous cluster of stars known as Capricorn, be thought to suggest the shape of any animal, let alone a goat?

It is more likely that the figures of the zodiac developed in a quite different way. They were taken from existing mythological symbols to which the shapes of the groups of stars were adjusted.

The Babylonians imagined that not only the Moon but also the Sun revolved around the Earth. They pictured these two great luminaries as playing a series of different roles as they passed through the different stages of their journey. It was as if they put on a different mask every time they entered a new constellation.

To illustrate how this principle worked in the naming of the constellations, let us take the sign of Aries, the Ram. The heavenly host was originally thought of as a flock of sheep with a ram (the Sun) as its leader. When the solar year of the Babylonians began in Aries, the brightest star of the constellation, Hamal, was thought of as a kind of replica of the Sun, opening the year in much the same way the Sun opened the day. It therefore became the Sun in his capacity as a ram. Originally the Ram was just the single star, Hamal, but later the surrounding stars were incorporated into the sign.

Geographical and meteorological factors also played a part in the formation of the zodiac. Aquarius, the Water-Pourer, for example, is the Sun in his capacity as a rain-giver. This is because of the heavy rainfall that occurred in Babylonia in January—the time when the Sun was in Aquarius.

The alternation of night and day is reflected in the way in which the constellation figures are associated alternately with the Sun and Moon, or night and day. Thus while the first sign, Aries, is a day sign, the second, Taurus, is a night sign. The horns of the Moon lead to an obvious association with those of a bull. And so the alternation continues round the zodiac. Today the division between day and night signs has been transformed into a division between positive and negative signs.

In this way the Babylonians built up the complicated celestial system which became the basis for their astrology.

One of the early astrological reports to the King of Babylon begins with the words:

'May there be peace to the King my lord. May Mercury and Jupiter to the King my lord be propitious. Long days, soundness of flesh and joy of heart may the gods to the King my lord grant!'[1]

There follows a long discussion of the likely meteorological effects of certain planetary phenomena. This report is typical of the early Babylonian astrology which was used only to predict events of a general nature such as floods, bad harvests, rebellions, wars, and so on. At this stage it was still a fairly crude and unsophisticated system. But between 600 and 300 BC it took a completely new step, moving from the old, general astrology of the *Enuma Anu Ellil* to a new and more precise kind. It was during this period that the first individual birth horoscopes were cast.

There are, in existence, a number of the stone tablets, in-

[1] *Reports of the Magicians and Astrologers of Nineveh and Babylon.* Ed. R. C. Thomson.

scribed with cuneiform writing, on which the Babylonians recorded their horoscope readings. These are the only primary evidence we have of Babylonian horoscope-casting. All other evidence comes to us through Greek and Roman writers of a very much later period. However, the few cuneiform horoscopes that do exist provide very valuable evidence of early Babylonian horoscopy. Here, for example, is an extract from a horoscope cast for a man named Aristokrates in the year 234 BC:

'The position of Jupiter means that his life will be regular. He will become rich and will grow old. The position of Venus means that wherever he may go it will be favourable for him. Mercury in Gemini means that he will have sons and daughters.'[1]

The basic principles of horoscope astrology were set down by these early Babylonian priests and have remained essentially the same over the centuries. It is the system they invented, plus a few additions, that astrologers use today.

It was also in Babylonian times that there emerged the system of elements which became such an important part of modern astrology. The Babylonians worshipped, as either kindly or malevolent powers, the Earth, whether fruitful or barren, the waters that fertilise or devastate, the winds which blow from the four points of the horizon, and the fire which burns and devours.

The Jews were one of the groups influenced by the Assyrio-Babylonian astrologers, or 'Chaldeans' as they later came to be called. Not long after the Jews left Egypt they were met by Balaam, a Chaldean of Pethor in Mesopotamia. After thrice building seven altars he prophesied (Numbers xxiv, 17) that: 'There shall come a Star out of Jacob, and a sceptre shall rise out of Israel, and shall smite the corners of Moab and destroy all the children of Seth'—a statement which has been interpreted as foretelling the coming of Christ. Another astrological reference is to be found in Judges v, 20: 'They fought from heaven; the stars in their courses fought against Sisera.' And

[1] A. Sachs, 'Babylonian Horoscopes', *Journal of Cuneiform Studies*, Vol. VI.

again Amos advised his followers to: 'Seek him that maketh the seven stars in Orion, and turneth the shadow of death into the morning' (Amos v, 8). The Old Testament contains many more references to the star-worship of Israel.

Yet the attitude of the Jews towards astrology seems to have been mixed. Some of them evidently turned against the Babylonian influence in their religion, for Zephenia says: 'I will cut off the remnant of Baal from this place . . . and them that worship the host of heaven upon the housetops' (Zeph. i, 4–5). It seems that while the lower and cruder forms of star-worship were forbidden, most learned Jews nevertheless showed acquaintance with and respect for the higher principles of Chaldean astrology.[1] Later the more mystical-minded Jews were among the foremost exponents of astrology when it came to Europe.

One of the most remarkable instances of astrology in the Bible is the story of the Magi in the New Testament. It was no coincidence that the three wise men from the east were led to Jesus by a star. The star and what it portended were part of a very ancient Chaldean legend as we have seen from the prophecy in the book of Numbers. In Chaldean astrology the constellation of Cassiopeia is the one which presides over Syria and Palestine. This constellation was known as 'The Woman with Child' because every three hundred years or so it brought forth an unusually bright star. To an astrologer, the appearance of the star would mean that the Queen of Palestine had brought forth an heir to the throne. If this were the case it would be of the utmost importance to go and pay homage to the future king. It has been calculated that it was this star which appeared just after the birth of Christ and must, therefore, have been the one which the Magi observed and followed.

Egyptian astrology

At the time when the Jews escaped from Egypt, their Egyptian captors knew little or nothing of astrology, though later they were to claim it as their own invention. The fact of the matter

[1] W. G. Collingwood, *Astrology in the Apocalypse*.

is that astrology did not come to Egypt until the Persian conquests brought it there in the sixth century BC and did not really develop fully until the Hellenistic period. Nevertheless there was a type of star-lore in Egypt long before this.

The earliest Egyptian astronomical texts are found on coffin-lids of the Middle Kingdom period (ie circa 2100–1800 BC). These give evidence of a very crude astronomical system, partly religious and partly practical in character, and entirely lacking in the mathematical sophistication of the Babylonians. The Egyptians did, however, possess one valuable invention, the Egyptian calendar. The fact that this calendar was invented primarily for agricultural purposes and bore little relation to astronomical factors is possibly the reason for its simplicity. Each year consisted of twelve months of thirty days each, and at the end of the year five days were added to make up the full complement. This was infinitely preferable to the Babylonian lunar calendar with its complicated intercalations. It was understandable, therefore, that it was adopted enthusiastically by the Greek astronomers. In pointing out the superiority of the Egyptian calendar, Neugebauer says that:

'It is a serious problem to determine the number of days between two given Babylonian or Greek new year's days, say fifty years apart. In Egypt this interval is simply fifty times 365. No wonder that the Egyptian calendar became the standard astronomical system of reference which was kept alive through the Middle Ages and was still used by Copernicus.'[1]

Another Egyptian contribution was the division of the day and night into twelve parts each. In ancient Egyptian times the day was defined as the interval between sunrise and sunset. This period, like the night, had to be divided into twelve equal parts. Thus the length of the hours varied depending on the time of year. At the height of the summer, for instance, the day-hours would be very long and the night-hours very short. This system became obsolete only when the mechanical clock was invented.

[1] Neugebauer, *The Exact Sciences in Antiquity*, Ch. 4.

As far as astrology is concerned, the only Egyptian invention of any importance was that of the decans. Originally these were constellations whose rising occurred ten days apart from one another—hence the name. They were also used to measure time during the night. Later, under Greek influence, these decans were incorporated into the Babylonian zodiac, so that each sign was divided into three decans of ten degrees each. The Egyptian deities governing the decans were also incorporated into the system.

The theme that is repeated throughout the Egyptian zodiac is the conflict between the two opposing forces of, on the one hand, light, knowledge and goodness; and on the other, darkness, ignorance and evil. As in Babylonian astrology, the darkness is usually represented by a serpent. The conquering force of light, on the other hand, is represented by the ibis- or hawk-headed figure familiar in Egyptian mythology.

One of the kings of Egypt in the Hellenistic period, Ptolemy III (246–221 BC), was a firm believer in astrology as is shown by a bizarre story connected with his wife Berenice. Soon after their marriage, Ptolemy was obliged to go and fight in Syria, and his wife vowed that she would sacrifice her hair, famous for its beauty, if only he would return safely. She kept her vow and when the king returned he was furious to find his wife minus her hair. His anger was directed towards the priests who declared that the hair had mysteriously disappeared during the night. To abate the king's rage, one of the court astronomers backed up the story by announcing that he had discovered in the sky a new constellation, 'the hair of Berenice'. Evidently the story took hold, for the name of the constellation persists to this day.

Ancient American astrology

Before leaving the subject of the early origins of astrology it is worth mentioning the astrology of the ancient civilisations of Central and South America. As far as we know, this was a completely isolated phenomenon, having no connection with the development of astrology in Babylonia.

Yet it has been said that the ancient Maya, who flourished in what is now Mexico from about AD 300, had a knowledge of astronomy even more accurate than that of the Babylonians. Like their Middle Eastern counterparts, the Maya had a sect of priest-astronomers who observed the sky from the tops of huge pyramids, not unlike those built by the Egyptians. They had a calendar of 365 days, only a fraction less than the amount of time required for the Sun to go round the Earth.

Venus was one of the heavenly bodies most revered by the Maya and they called it by various names including 'Nohek' (the great star) and 'Xux ek' (the wasp star). They worked out a calendar for the movements of Venus over a period of 384 years. It has also been suggested that the Maya had their own zodiac which contained thirteen instead of twelve signs.[1]

The Aztecs, too, venerated the heavens, though their astronomical system was much cruder than that of the Maya. Like the ancient Egyptians they thought in terms of a perpetual war fought between the forces of light and darkness, heat and cold, north and south. Correspondingly, the stars were grouped into armies of the east and of the west.

Like the Maya they had a calendrical year which differed fractionally from the solar year and therefore had to be brought into line with the solar year after an established period had elapsed. This bringing into line was the occasion for a strange ceremony. At the end of one calendrical period of years and before the beginning of the next, the priests ascended a hill and scanned the horizon, awaiting the hour when certain stars, probably Aldebaran or the Pleiades, reached the centre of the heavens and gave the sign that the world was to continue. At the very moment when these stars passed the meridian, the priests seized a wooden fire-drill and kindled a new fire in the open breast of a freshly slain victim. Great rejoicing among the population followed.[2]

The interest of the Aztecs and the Maya in cosmology is shown by a curious ball game which is believed to have originated as early as 800 BC, ie, long before the Mayan civilisa-

[1] S. G. Morley, *The Ancient Maya.*
[2] G. C. Vaillant, *The Aztecs of Mexico.*

tion, and which was witnessed by conquistadores in the sixteenth century. It was played with a solid rubber ball on a court shaped like a capital I, between two teams of about five each, the object being to make the ball pass through a stone ring fixed to the side wall.

According to Indian legend, the game was originally played in the sky by the gods who used the stars as balls. As played by the Maya and Aztecs, the game had cosmological significance. The court represented the world, and the ball either the Sun or Moon. The movements of the ball could be used to make predictions. The game also symbolised the constant struggle between light and dark and was sometimes accompanied by human sacrifice.

Unfortunately the great civilisations of America were cut off in the bud following the Spanish and Portuguese invasions and they ceased to have any significant influence on the world. Fascinating as they were, they are of no further interest to the historian of astrology.

We therefore return to Europe to take up our story as the heritage of the Babylonians passes on to other civilisations.

If the Babylonians invented the substance of astrology, it was the Greeks who gave it form. By bringing to it their unique intellectual gifts, they bestowed on it the structure which has enabled it to survive ever since.

The Greek contribution to astrology may seem surprising to those who look upon Greek thought as the antithesis of all that is arcane and mysterious, and to whom the word 'Greek' is almost synonymous with 'calmly rational'. But the irrational and mystical side of man's nature has a habit of flourishing on the soil of reason and throughout the history of Greek thought and religion there run the two contrasting currents of logic and superstition. While the city-states officially worshipped the gay, anthropomorphic gods of the Olympian pantheon, the country populations often displayed allegiance to more sinister and mysterious creeds of oriental origin.

Long before the age of Alexander, which brought the Greeks into direct contact with the Chaldeans, there was, on the Greek peninsula, evidence of certain mystical cults which boasted a considerable following. One example of such a cult is that of Mithraism which came originally from Persia. It was a mystery cult whose followers passed through seven stages of initiation, each one representing part of the soul's journey through the seven planetary realms to the outermost realm or 'seventh

c

heaven'. In the rites connected with the cult, the celebrants wore masks representing the animals of the zodiac.[1]

A similar cult, believed to be related to Mithraism, was that of the Eleusinian Mysteries which were based on the legend of Demeter and Persephone. Public rites were carried out at Eleusis and thousands of people were initiated there every year.

At the same time as astrology was beginning to make itself felt through these mystery religions, the philosophers were busy speculating about the nature and meaning of the heavens. The most widely held view was that the Earth was surrounded by a series of concentric spheres, each one enveloping the other. There were seven spheres ruled by the seven planets and an eighth and outermost sphere to which the stars were fixed.

How many of these theories were derived from oriental astrology is difficult to know, but it is certain that the oriental influence on Greek thought began very early. The Belgian ancient historian, Franz Cumont, points out that:

> 'At a distant date Hellas received from the East, a duo-decimal or sexagesimal system of measurement. The habit of reckoning in terms of twelve hours . . . is due to the fact that the Ionians borrowed from the orientals this method of dividing the day. Besides the acquaintance with early instruments such as the sun-dial, they owed to the observatories of Mesopotamia the fundamental data of their celestial topography: the ecliptic, the signs of the zodiac and the majority of the planets.'[2]

The original Greek names for the planets were based purely on their appearance and character. The bright planet Venus was called 'Herald of the Dawn' or 'Herald of Light' and some-times 'Vespertine' or 'Star of the Evening'; Mercury was called the 'Twinkling Star'; Mars, the 'Fiery Star' on account of its red colour; Jupiter, the 'Luminous Star'; and Saturn, the 'Brilliant Star' or the 'Indicator'. After the fourth century BC,

[1] Joseph Campbell, *The Masks of God*, Vol. III, Ch. 6.
[2] Franz Cumont, *Astrology and Religion among the Greeks and Romans*, II.

however, these names were replaced by the names of Greek deities. Mercury became Hermes; Venus, Aphrodite; Jupiter, Zeus; and Saturn, Kronos. This does not indicate any connection between the Olympian pantheon and astrology. (The names were chosen purely because those gods bore a certain resemblance to the Babylonian deities who were thought to govern the planets.) These were, respectively, Nabu, Ishtar, Nergal, Marduk and Ninib.

One of the philosophers whose writings show the influence of sidereal religion is Plato. He spoke of two different kinds of love. 'To understand both varieties of love,' he explained in the *Symposium*, 'in relation to the revolutions of the heavenly bodies and seasons of the year, is termed astronomy.' He called the stars 'divine and eternal animals ever abiding'.

Aristotle held similar views. To him, the stars appeared as purer forms of life which exerted their influence upon the life of the earth. He also held a theory that there were a number of lesser gods who were ruled by the planetary spheres, a thought which was to crop up later in many different disguises.

Some very interesting ideas were developed through the theory held by certain Greek philosophers that there was a connection between the motions of the planets and music. They discovered that a musical scale depended on relations of numbers and they tried to prove that the motions of the heavenly bodies were related to one another in the same way as numbers in a harmony.

There were three musical consonances known to the Greeks: the diapason, or octave, in the proportion of two to one; the diapent, or fifth, in that of three to two; and the diateseron, or fourth, in that of four to three. The scale was completed by the addition of the semitones and of the tones filling in the intervals between the consonances.

Pythagoras, who discovered these relations, also developed an entire harmonic cosmography, the exposition of which is set out in a treatise by Timaeus of Locris.

The Greeks believed that the motion of a body was a measure of the quantity of its soul. To determine the relative degrees of velocity (and therefore soul) of the planets, they imagined a straight line drawn from the Earth to the outermost sphere. This they divided according to the proportions of the musical scale, and on this scale the various planets were arranged. Saturn, the outermost planet, corresponded to the thirty-sixth tone. The Earth corresponded to the first. In between, the other planets were set at varying harmonic distances.

Plato speaks in the *Republic* about this supposed musical harmony between the planets. Each of the spheres, he taught, carried within it a siren. When these sirens sounded together, each one emitting a different note, they formed a sublime celestial concert.[1]

In spite of the widespread influence in Greece of sidereal theology, it was a long time before the fatalistic aspects of astrology took hold and people began to use the science for the purposes of divination. After the time of Alexander, however, this situation changed and astrology came to be practised extensively among the Greeks.

The conquests of Alexander the Great and the establishing of the Hellenistic empire were of the utmost importance for the subsequent development of Western civilisation. In order to understand how astrology came to be disseminated after it left Babylon, it is necessary to appreciate the fundamental changes which took place at this time.

The conquests of Alexander the Great had three effects of supreme importance. The first was the breaking down of national barriers and the creation of a new international spirit in thought and religion. This was made possible by Alexander's reverence for the religions of his conquered countries and of his unprecedented respect for the rights of their citizens.

The second effect was the spread of the Greek tongue. Before Alexander's day Greece had never had a national language. Each separate city-state had its own dialect which was often incomprehensible to the inhabitants of the neighbouring state. And while there was no linguistic unity, it was impossible for Greece to exercise her intellectual influence on a large scale. But after the collapse of the city-states and the adoption of Greek by the Macedonians under Alexander, there

[1] Flammarion, *History of the Heavens*. Tr. J. F. Blake.

Babylonian stela of ninth century BC, set up in honour of a father by his son. The two are shown standing below the symbols of the planetary gods Shamash, Sin and Nergal

Assyrian instrument for making astrological calculations; from Nineveh; seventh century BC

Cameo of the Emperor Augustus, made of onyx of two different colours. Above the Emperor can be seen the symbol of his zodiacal sign, Capricorn

arose out of the multitude of dialects, a national Greek language which was intelligible to all Greeks and easy for foreigners to understand.

The third important consequence of Alexander's conquests was the bringing about of a blending of many different religions which laid the foundations for the development of eclectic cults like Hermeticism.

One of the conquered countries was Babylonia and there came to be a tremendous intellectual interchange between the two countries. Astrology is said to have been brought to Greece by a Chaldean priest called Berosus who established himself on the island of Cos around the year 280 BC and there revealed to his pupils the contents of various Babylonian cuneiform writings and astrological treatises. Another Chaldean, Soudines, was invited to the court of King Attalus I of Pergamus about the year 238 BC, where he practised various forms of divination including astrology.

The influence also flowed in the other direction and centres of Greek learning were established in Mesopotamia. This enabled Babylonian astrology to profit from the disciplines of the Greek philosophers and the discoveries of the Greek astronomers. In such an atmosphere of intellectual and religious interchange, astrology flourished and grew.

One of the Greek schools of thought which was affected by Babylonian astrology was that of Stoicism, the most important philosophical movement to appear in the Hellenic world and one whose influence continued until the time of its last great follower, the Emperor Marcus Aurelius.

The Stoics saw the world as an organism of sympathetic forces which acted and reacted incessantly upon one another, and they attributed a predominating influence to the heavenly bodies. This belief and their doctrine of infallible destiny made their theories very similar to the determinism of the Chaldeans. For this reason, the Stoic philosophy achieved tremendous success all over the semitic world as far as Mesopotamia. At the same time, Zeno, the founder of Stoicism, displays in his writings the influence of Chaldean astrology.

Another Hellenic philosopher who revered astrology was

Lucian of Samosata. He is credited with a treatise on the subject which he defends in these words:

'The stars follow their orbit in the heaven; but independently of their motion, they act upon what passes here below. If you admit that a horse in a gallop, that birds in flying and men in walking, make the stones jump or drive the little floating particles of dust by the wind of their course, why should you deny that the stars have any effect? The smallest fire sends us its emanations, and although it is not for us that the stars burn, and they care very little about warning us, why should we not receive any emanations from them? Astrology, it is true, cannot make that good which is evil. It can effect no change in the course of events, but it renders a service to those who cultivate it by announcing to them good things to come; it produces joy by anticipation at the same time that it fortifies them against evil. Misfortune, in fact, does not take them by surprise, the foreknowledge of it renders it easier and lighter. That is my way of looking at astrology.'[1]

Greek interest in the stars did not only take the form of Stoic mysticism. It was also seen in the investigations of certain Greek mathematicians who made many great discoveries in the field of astronomy. One of the most remarkable achievements was the discovery, credited to Aristarchus of Samos, who lived around 300 BC, of the heliocentric system. Departing from the accepted theory that the Earth was the centre of the universe, Aristarchus held that the Earth and planets moved around the Sun, the Earth revolving continuously on its own axis. The Sun and stars, he believed, remained fixed.

Understandably, this violent departure from the orthodox view of the time aroused bitter opposition from the Stoics, one of whom, Cleanthus, demanded that Aristarchus be brought to trial for his heresy. The removal of the Earth from the centre of the universe threatened the whole structure of Stoic cosmology and ethics, just as, a thousand years later, it was to threaten Christian cosmology and ethics.

[1] Lucian, *On Astrology*.

Another Greek mathematician, Eratosthenes of Alexandria, made a remarkably accurate estimate of the Earth's circumference. He also calculated the Moon's distance from the Earth fairly correctly and estimated the Sun's distance at half what it is known to be today.

Later, most of this knowledge was forgotten and was not to be rediscovered until the time of Copernicus and Galileo.

The Ptolemaic system

One of the countries that came under Greek intellectual hegemony was Egypt. Here astrology had been adopted during the Persian period in the sixth century BC, and when the Greeks entered the country they found that the Egyptians had already developed their own modified system of astrology which I mentioned in the first chapter. The presence of the Greeks in Egypt led to an extremely fertile combination of intellect and learning of which the great centre at Alexandria became the outstanding example.

It was at Alexandria that the Greek astronomer Ptolemy composed his treatises the *Almagest* and the *Tetrabiblos*. Ptolemy was the foremost astronomer of his time. Although his basic theories have now been disproved, nevertheless by his daring and original ideas on the movements of the heavenly bodies and the structure of the solar system he blazed the trail for later astronomers. The *Almagest*, which contained the essence of his astronomical teachings, continued in use for four hundred years as the highest authority in astronomical matters.

Ptolemy, like most astronomers of his time, took it for granted that the stars were capable of influencing human lives. Though this belief formed a separate department of his subject it was nevertheless a natural extension of his activities as an astronomer. What we would now call the astrological side of his teaching is set out in his *Tetrabiblos*. Because of its unequalled influence on the subsequent development of astrology, it would be worth while to outline the doctrine contained in this book.[1]

[1] For my summary I have used J. M. Ashmand's translation.

As its name implies, the work is set out in four books. Ptolemy begins Book I by establishing the premises for his belief in stellar influence. The earth, he says, is surrounded by 'a certain power derived from aetherial nature' which is diffused over and pervades the whole atmosphere of the Earth, and which Ptolemy refers to as the 'Ambient'. This is the vehicle by which planetary and stellar forces are transmitted.

For evidence of these forces Ptolemy points to the obvious influence of the Sun and Moon, the former causing seasonal changes and variations in temperature, the latter affecting the tides. He then makes a rather illogical jump to the assertion that the stars also have physical effects. 'They cause heats, winds, and storms, to the influence of which earthly things are conformably subjected.' He then continues:

> 'From these premises, it follows not only that all bodies, which may be already compounded, are subjected to the motion of the stars, but also that the impregnation and growth of the seeds from which all bodies proceed, are formed and moulded by the quality existing in the ambient at the time of such impregnation and growth.'

It follows, Ptolemy goes on, that if a person is able to foresee the relative positions of the Sun, Moon, planets and stars at a given time, and at the same time is familiar with the character of each heavenly body, then he will be able to predict certain things about the time in question.

Ptolemy goes on to enumerate the uses of prognostication among which he includes the curing of physical ailments by 'Medical Mathematics'. 'It is by this process', he says, 'that remedies for the present and preservations against future disorders are to be acquired: for without astronomical knowledge, medical aid would be most frequently unavailing.'

The rest of Book I Ptolemy devotes to an exposition of the basic tools of his astrological system. For example, he divides the planets into benefics and malefics and attributes various qualities to them such as heat, cold, dryness and moisture. He also explains the different characteristics of the various signs and houses. All this he seems to take for granted as part of the astrological tradition.

In Book II Ptolemy comes to the practical application of his system. He begins by discussing what he calls 'general' or 'universal' astrology, which concerns entire nations or cities rather than individuals. He makes some interesting statements about the astrological causes of certain national characteristics. He says, for example, that:

> 'The natives of those countries which lie towards the east excel in courage, acting boldly and openly under all circumstances; for in all their characteristics they are principally conformed to the Sun's nature, which is oriental, diurnal, masculine and dexter.'

In another chapter he states that: 'Britain, Galatia, Germany and Barsania have a greater share of familiarity with Aries and Mars; and their inhabitants are accordingly wilder, bolder and more ferocious.' From this astro-geographical knowledge, Ptolemy holds, it is possible to determine how different parts of the world will be affected by any given astronomical event.

In the last two books, Ptolemy deals with the individual horoscope, discussing in Book III the factors that influence an individual from within himself, and in Book IV those that influence him from without.

In Book III he gives detailed instructions as to how an enquiry concerning an individual should be carried out:

> 'Firstly notice must be taken of that place in the zodiac which corresponds . . . with the particular division of the inquiry . . . [eg the individual's health, marriage, duration of life, or whatever].
>
> Secondly, after the proper place has been duly ascertained, the planets holding right of dominion there . . . are to be observed . . .
>
> Thirdly, the natures of the ruling planet and of the signs, in which itself and the place which it thus controls may severally be situated, are to be considered as indicating the quality of the event.

Fourthly, the proportionate vigour and strength, or weakness, with which the dominion is exercised, as exhibited either by the actual cosmical position in the scheme of the nativity, will point out to what extent and with what force the event will operate . . .

Lastly, the general time, about which the event will take place, is to be inferred from the ruling planet's matutine or vespertine position . . .'

It is interesting to note the way in which Ptolemy allots the various planets to different departments of human life, for most of the correspondences that he set down passed into later astrological tradition. 'The Sun and Saturn', he says, 'are allotted to the person of the father; and the Moon and Venus to that of the mother.' Further on he says that:

'Of the spiritual qualities . . . all those which are national and intellectual are contemplated by the situation of Mercury; while all others, which regard the mere sensitive faculties, and are independent of reason, are considered rather by other luminaries of a less subtle constitution and a more ponderous body; for instance, by the Moon and such stars as she may be configured with.'

In the fourth and final book Ptolemy deals with factors affecting the individual from outside himself, for example wealth, rank, employment and marriage. All these have their planetary correspondences and the method used is similar to that set out in Book III.

The methods of interpretation expounded in the *Tetrabiblos* undoubtedly derived from earlier astrological tradition, but a person of Ptolemy's intellect would not have set them down as fact unless he had satisfied himself that there was at least some empirical truth in them. Even if one does not accept Ptolemy's theories, they are of enormous historical interest and continue to influence astrologers today.

Astrology in the Trismegistic writings

Influential though it was, Ptolemy's work was of an objective, scientific nature and would never have exercised the influence it did had it not been for the religious climate of the time in which astrology flourished. The real inspiration of the astrologers came not from scientific theories but from certain mystical treatises in which astrology had an important status.

Egypt was the birth-place of a number of these occult works. About the year 150 BC, there were composed in Greek at Alexandria the writings attributed to the priest Petosiris and his king, Nechepso. Petosiris is supposed to have had a historical basis in an Egyptian philosopher who wrote on comparative Greek and Egyptian theology and treated of astrology and the Egyptian mysteries. His revelations to the mythical King Nechepso became the sacred books of the growing faith in the stars.[1] They were later to have an influence on Roman astrologers like Vettius Valens.

Another important body of mystical lore, composed in Egypt between 50 BC and AD 150, was the collection of writings attributed to Hermes Trismegistos. Hermes was the Greek version of the Egyptian god Thoth (Tehuti), who, in Egypt, became the revealer of the wisdom of the astrologers. The Greek title, Trismegistos, means 'thrice-great'.

Cumont points out that:

'It was a difficult task to reconcile astrology with national beliefs as Hermeticism sought to do. For astrology was not only a method of divination; it implied a religious conception of the world, and it was inseparably combined with Greek philosophy. Thus the Hermetic books comprise not merely treatises on learned superstition; it is a complete theology that the gods teach to the faithful in a series of apocalypses.'[2]

These writings were to have a marked influence on certain early Christians.

[1] Franz Cumont, *Astrology and Religion among the Greeks and Romans*, III.
[2] Ibid.

'The early Church fathers in general accepted the Trisme-gistic writings as exceedingly ancient and authoritative, and in their apologetic writings quote them in support of the main general propositions of Christianity.'[1]

An illustration of the importance accorded to astrology in the Trismegistic writings appears in a text in which Asclepius, the mythical disciple of Hermes, is revealing certain truths to King Ammon of Egypt. After expounding with great enthusiasm on the power and grandeur of the Sun, Asclepius says to the king:

'And under Him [the Sun] is ranged the choir of daimons —or rather, choirs; for these are multitudinous and very varied, ranked underneath the groups of Stars, in equal number with each one of them.

So, marshalled in their ranks, they are the ministers of each one of the Stars, being in their natures good, and bad, that is, in their activities (for that a daimon's essence is activity); while some of them are (of) mixed (natures), good and bad.

To all of these has been allotted the authority o'er things upon the Earth; and it is they who bring about the multifold confusion of the turmoils on the Earth—for states and nations generally, and for each individual separately.'[2]

Here is a repetition of the Aristotelian doctrine of lesser gods ruled by the spheres of the planets. We are to see it re-appearing later in the theories of the medieval demonologists.

The Greek synthesis

By the time astrology came to be passed from Greece to Rome, the Bablylonian, Egyptian and Greek elements had crystallised into a single unified system. At this stage it would be useful to outline the fundamental principles of the astrology that had emerged from this fusion.

We have seen how the planets and the signs of the zodiac

[1] G. R. S. Mead, *Thrice-Greatest Hermes*, Vol. I, Ch. 2.
[2] Ibid. Vol. II, the *Corpus Hermeticum*, XVI.

S pricht Althabicius das ☿ sig ein ver
mister planet vnd ein menlicher vnd ey
teglicher vnd wirt sin nattur geneigt
durcch die anderen planeten. Dann ist
er by einem gutten So ist sin natur auch gut
Ist er bey einem bösen So ist sin nattur auch
böß. Ist er aber by einem nichtigen So ist sin
natur auch nichtig Ist er tegig So ist sin
nattur auch tegig Vnd hatt zubediutte
die kleineren brüder Dorum sich in yomas
gebirtt wie sich ☿ hab mit dem herren des
ersten oder mit dem diutter der gebirtt Wan

A page from a fifteenth-century German edition of Guido Bonatti's
Liber Astronomicus: Mercury, the planet of learning, above his
two signs of Gemini and Virgo

Es spricht Althabicius das ♂ sig ein melich planet ein nechtlicher planet vnd ein bose vnd wirckt durch sin nattur hitz vnd dúrre on temperment vnd ist fúrig vnd bitters geschmacks vnd der complexion die man nent Colericam vnd ist nattúrlichen eyn bedútter der brieder vnd der vetter vnd dorúm ist ♂ Nattúrliche ein bedútter der brieder warm die brúeder sind der dritt zúfal das dem kind zúfalt nach der empfengt núß das ist nach der gebúrt vnd das do das kind mir liep hatt vnder denen die in vorhin mogen zú

Another page from *Liber Astronomicus*: Mars, the warrior, with Aries and Scorpio

fitted into the system. The other main concept of horoscope astrology was that of the twelve houses. Whereas the signs are imaginary divisions of the sky, the houses are imaginary divisions of the Earth's surface projected into the sky. The cusp of the first house is formed by the *ascendant*, that is to say the eastern point of the horizon. This point passes through a new sign every two hours and the sign in which it falls at the time of birth is still regarded by astrologers as of fundamental importance in determining the person's character. Besides the ascendant, there are three other cardinal points at ninety-degree intervals round the Earth; these are the descendant (western horizon), the mid-heaven (directly overhead), and the lower mid-heaven (directly below).

The part played by the houses in relation to the signs and planets can be explained as follows. (The planets represent the basic forces that come into play on a person's character; the signs indicate the ways in which these forces are modified in the way that rays of light are modified when they pass through coloured panes of stained glass; finally, the houses show the earthly sectors, or departments, of everyday life in which the modified forces operate.)

The houses were originally eight in number, but were later extended to twelve. Their characteristics, like those of the signs, have changed little in astrological theory over the centuries.

Another idea that was fully developed by this time was that of each of the planets 'ruling' one or two of the signs. The Sun and Moon are said to rule Leo and Cancer respectively, while Mercury, Mars, Venus, Jupiter and Saturn rule, in corresponding order, the following pairs: Virgo and Gemini, Aries and Scorpio, Taurus and Libra, Sagittarius and Pisces, Capricorn and Aquarius.

Some of these rulerships are of Greek and others of Babylonian origin. Eisler suggests that the rulership of Venus in Libra is connected with the legend of the goddess seeing Adonis rise from Hades and sink down again at the autumn equinox, coinciding with the Sun in Libra, while her rulership in Taurus is linked with the story of Zeus assuming the form of a bull when he pursued his love affair with Europa. He also suggests, more obviously, that Mars was made to rule Aries because of the ram's supposed qualities of aggressiveness, and Scorpio because of the animal's venomous sting.[1]

The planets were divided into those that were friendly and those that were unfriendly, now referred to as 'benefics' and 'malefics'. The Sun and Moon, Jupiter and Venus were benefics; Mars and Saturn were malefics; while Mercury could take on either aspect, depending on the planets and signs with which it was associated.

A further elaboration of the system was the theory of aspects. The aspect of one planet to another is the angle formed by two lines drawn from the centre of a chart to the points on the perimeter where the planets are placed. If the planets are exactly opposite one another they are said to be in 'opposition', or if they coincide they are in 'conjunction'. Other important aspects are trine (120 degrees), sextile (60 degrees) and square (90 degrees). The aspects were regarded by the Greeks as of great importance in that they modified the ways in which the forces of the planets were exercised.

At this time there was already a distinction between fatalistic and catarchic astrology. The former assumed that a person's future was predetermined down to the last detail by the positions of the heavenly bodies at the time of birth. The latter regarded the stars as influencing only certain sections of a person's life. Thus the catarchic astrologer believed that he was able to advise his client on the most auspicious times for carrying out certain undertakings on the assumption that 'forewarned is forearmed'.

The Greek astronomer Hipparchus made a discovery that was to play havoc with astrological theory. As we have seen in Babylonian and in early Greek astronomy and astrology the signs of the zodiac were connected not only with the seasons of the year but also with the actual groups of stars that were visible at the point where the sun rose at the season in question. The sign of Aries was believed to be fixed to the spring equinox. What Hipparchus discovered was that the spring

[1] Robert Eisler, *The Royal Art of Astrology*, Ch. 23.

equinox was not fixed in relation to the ecliptic, but moved slowly round it at the rate of about one sign in every two thousand years. Thus, the spring equinox is today in Pisces and will quite soon be entering Aquarius. Since this discovery was made, the signs of the zodiac, in astrological terminology, have been fixed to the equinoxes and are unrelated to the constellations they once represented.

The Greek passion for science and learning, that was later to transmit its light to the Roman world, owed a great deal to astrology. The idea of the celestial bodies as intelligences governing human fate, and the possibility of interpreting their movements by diligent observation, were a tremendous inspiration to the enquiring mind of the Greeks. In astrology the objectivity of science and the mystical passion of religion were united in one study.

Babylon, the country which had sown the seeds of so much learning, had eventually come to its tragic end in the second century BC. Overrun successively by the Parthians and the Syrians, and reconquered by King Phraates of Mesopotamia, Babylon was subjected to terrible ravages for a quarter of a century. Finally the city was sacked and burned in 125 BC and the remains of a great civilisation finally perished. But the intellectual heritage of Babylon was far from dead. Astrology, reinforced by the Greeks, was to pass on to the next great empire to dominate the west, Rome.

Chapter 3   The Roman world

Astrology's conquest of Rome

The story of astrology among the Romans is as colourful and as turbulent as the history of Rome itself. Although its influence started earlier, it came to Rome in full force in the second century BC along with the Hellenising influences which followed the second Punic War, and began to exercise a strong influence on Roman life and thought. As with the Greeks, this influence was felt in three different ways. In the first place it was felt at its most overt through the activities of the soothsayers and diviners who professed to use 'Chaldean' astrological methods. Secondly it was felt in the works of certain Roman poets and thinkers who were inspired by astrological symbolism. Thirdly, astrology had its effect on the religious life of Rome and astrological ideas are clearly discernible in most of the cults which flourished in Rome and throughout the empire.

The divinatory aspect of astrology is perhaps the least important of the three, but it is worth discussing in view of the large number of people who followed the advice of the diviners and because of the many bizarre incidents provoked by the practice.

It is worth explaining at this stage that the term 'Chaldean', as used by the Romans, was a somewhat vague one. In Babylonian times it had originally meant an inhabitant of Chaldea, or lower Mesopotamia, and was later used of the Babylonian priesthood as a whole. In Hellenic times it was a title conferred on Greeks who had studied in Babylonian schools. Finally it came to be used of anyone who claimed to be able to tell the future according to the stars. It was this last use which prevailed in Rome.

The beginnings of astrological influence in Rome can be traced to the days of the Republic which, as early as 300 BC, began to be infiltrated by oriental cults, some of which had astrological elements.

Cramer points out that by the middle of the third century BC, the influence of astrology was already apparent in the use of words like *considerare*, a compound of the word *sidus*, a star. The word, which has passed into our language, means literally to put the stars together, that is, examine their relative positions. Cramer also quotes a passage written by the comedy-writer Plautus (approx. 253–184 BC) in his *Rudens* in which he makes the star Arcturus say:

'Arcturus is my name. At night I shine in the sky amidst the host of gods, at daytime I wander about on earth among mortals. Other stars too descend to earth.

Jove, Lord of gods and men, sends us throughout the world, one this way, one elsewhere so that we might espy the deeds of men, their conduct, piety, and loyalty, and what use they make of riches.'[1]

The first great Roman scholar (as opposed to scholars of Greek origin) to profess and practise astrology was Publius Nigidius Figulus (approx. 99–45 BC). He was a close friend and political ally of Cicero, though the two held opposing views on astrology. Nigidius, as well as being a prolific writer on science, astrology, history and religion, also pursued a moderately successful career in politics until his views brought him into conflict with the recently self-appointed dictator, Julius Caesar, who sent him into exile. Cicero, who continued to

Frederick H. Cramer, *Astrology in Roman Law and Politics*, Ch. 2.

D

enjoy Caesar's favour, promised to intercede on his friend's behalf. But Nigidius died before Cicero was able to help.

Nigidius became the Roman apostle of the school known as Pythagoreanism which incorporated all the doctrines of fatalism inherent in astrology. His most lasting work consisted of two books, one on each of the two main constellation systems of the ancient world, the *Sphaera Barbarica* and the *Sphaera Graecanica*. The oriental system of the former was soon to be replaced by the latter. Thus Nigidius's book constituted a valuable record.

Nigidius enjoyed an awesome reputation as a diviner and many stories are told about him, some no doubt apocryphal. One says that on the day that the future Emperor Augustus was born, the child's father, a senator, arrived late at the assembly because of the happy event. As soon as he had delivered his explanation, Nigidius stood up and predicted, from the positions of the planets at that hour, that the newborn child would grow up to be a ruler.

Nigidius's friend Marcus Tullius Cicero (106–43 BC) was one of the last great opponents of astrology before the art of the stars took Rome by storm. It appears that in his early days, Cicero may have been friendly towards astrology, for in his poem *On My Consulate*, which he wrote after he had held the office in 63 BC, he made the muse Urania address him as follows:

> 'And when you should wish to learn the motions and straying orbits of the planets, which are located in the seat of the constellations . . . then you will already behold everything revealed by a divine spirit.'[1]

By the time he came to write *de Divinatione*, however, Cicero had turned firmly against astrology. In the book he delivers a diatribe against all forms of divination, including astrology. In doing so he was following the earlier example of Panaetius (born 190 BC), one of the few Stoics to oppose astrology, and of the diehard anti-Hellene Marcus Porcius Cato (234–149 BC) who had forbidden the overseer of his estate to consult 'Chaldeans'

[1] Quoted by Cramer. Ibid.

These opponents of astrology were, however, fighting a losing battle, for the art steadily gained ground.

From early on the political atmosphere of Rome favoured the growth of astrology and other methods of divination. The long period of revolution and political turbulence from the Gracchi to Julius Caesar, with its sudden 'reversals of fortune', prompted the belief in an ungovernable destiny.[1] Later its use to determine the fates of leaders became such a common practice that the emperors came to regard it as a threat to their security.

One of the early emperors who believed in astrology was Octavian, or Augustus as he proclaimed himself soon after ascending the throne. His conversion is said to have taken place some time before his ascent. The story goes that he was persuaded by his friend Agrippa to accompany the latter on a visit to the astrologer Theagenes. Having cast Agrippa's horoscope, Theagenes foretold astonishing prosperity for him, and Octavian, jealous of his friend's good fortune, refused at first to tell the astrologer his birth date. Eventually, when curiosity got the better of him, he agreed, and no sooner had Theagenes learned the necessary details about Octavian's birth than he threw himself at the latter's feet and worshipped him as the future master of the empire. Octavian was delighted and from then on was a firm believer in astrology. Later he had the emblem of his sign, Capricorn, struck on some of the coins that were issued in his reign.[2]

Yet despite Augustus's belief in astrology, it was under his reign, in 33 BC, that Agrippa, who was then aedile (the Roman magistrate superintending public works), ordered the 'astrologers and magicians' to be expelled from Rome. If Augustus believed in astrology, we must conclude that the motives for this expulsion were political. Augustus had a firm belief in the accuracy of astrological prognostications and he may have feared that a prediction of his death or the advent of another emperor might precipitate an insurrection against him.

Augustus's successor, Tiberius, suffered from the same fear.

[1] H. W. Garrod, intr. to *Manilii Astronomicon II*.
[2] Flammarion, *History of the Heavens*. Tr. J. F. Blake.

Under his reign, many people were put to death for having cast their horoscopes to find out what honours were in store for them. But in secret Tiberius cast the horoscopes of great people to find out if he had any rivalry to fear.[1]

It is related that when he held these secret consultations, he often ordered the astrologer to be thrown into the sea afterwards, if he was suspected of indiscretion or treachery. After one consultation with an astrologer named Thrasyllus, the emperor asked him if he had cast his (Thrasyllus's) own horoscope and what signs were shown for himself for that day and hour. Thrasyllus examined the positions of the planets and as he did so he grew pale. Then, trembling with fear, he announced that he was very near his death. Tiberius then congratulated him on having escaped a danger by foreseeing it and henceforth admitted him to his most intimate circle of friends.[2]

Nero, before proclaiming himself emperor, is reported to have waited until a favourable time indicated by the 'Chaldeans' before he did so. Acting under the advice of the astrologer Balbillus, he avoided the disaster indicated by an inauspicious comet, by ordering a number of people to be executed as a human sacrifice.[3]

Domitian, like Tiberius before him, examined the horoscopes of prominent citizens and put to death one Metius Pompusianus who was reputed to have an 'imperial nativity'.[4] He also arrested a certain Ascletarion for predicting events unfavourable to the emperor. He asked the culprit what form his own death would take and was told that he would soon be torn to pieces by dogs. Domitian ordered the man to be put to death immediately, but in order to demonstrate the futility of his art, instructed that he should be buried with the greatest care. The executioners carried out his orders by burning the body; but as this was being done, a hurricane overturned the pyre and dogs devoured the half-burned corpse.[5]

[1] Ibid.
[2] Ibid.
[3] Suetonius, *Nero*, 36 and 40.
[4] Suetonius, *Titus*, 9.
[5] Suetonius, *Domitian*, 14.

Septimus Severus, who had lost his wife and wished to marry again, studied the horoscopes of a number of eligible ladies. To his disappointment none was encouraging. Eventually he learned that living in Syria was a young woman who had been told by the Chaldeans that she would one day be the wife of a king. At this time Commodus was emperor and Severus was still only a legate. He demanded and obtained her as his wife. Later wishing to test the truth of the prediction about her, he went to Sicily to consult a well-known astrologer. When Commodus heard of this treachery he was furious. Fortunately, Commodus was killed before he could take action and Severus, according to the prediction, became emperor.[1]

Such instances are many and various. Throughout the Roman Empire, the diviners and astrologers continued to practise their arts in spite of the fearful persecution which this often entailed.

Astrology in Roman literature and religion

From its first appearance in Rome, astrology was the subject of much controversy among the intelligentsia. The two great philosophical movements which flourished in Rome at this time were opposed in their views on astrology. The Stoics, with the notable exception of Panaetius, upheld the claims of the art. The Epicureans, on the other hand, rejected them vehemently. In the conflict between these two movements, it was stoicism which ultimately prevailed, in a triumph which was also a victory for astrology. The ultimate success of stoicism was due in large measure to the influence of the philosopher Posidonius, a figure of great importance in the philosophical and religious development of the Graeco-Roman world. The support which he gave to astrology was a considerable factor in its subsequent success among intellectuals.

Posidonius was born at Apamea in Syria around the year 135 BC, and after a long period of travel settled in the island of Rhodes where he set up a school. Unfortunately, his works are

Suetonius, *Severus*, 3.

almost entirely lost, but we do know quite a lot about his teachings from the writings of his many distinguished pupils who included Cicero and Pompey. As a great eclectic thinker, he drew on a wide variety of sources, including astrology, which played an important part in his system. As Cumont says, 'It was due to him that astrology entered into a coherent explanation of the world, acceptable to the most enlightened intellects, and that it was solidly based on a general theory of nature, from which it was to remain inseparable.'[1] His ideas were to have a powerful influence lasting as long as a century after his death. They are evident in the works of Seneca and in those of the astrologer Nigidius Figulus.

But the most important piece of literature which he inspired is the *Astronomics* of Manilius, a series of verses which constitute a lengthy and complex treatise on astrology. About the poet himself, almost nothing is known and even the name 'Manilius' was not his real name. The verses, which were written under the reign of Augustus, are one of the most interesting examples of a piece of literature inspired by astrology. Not only are they a remarkable piece of writing from a literary point of view, but they also constitute a valuable summary of Roman astrological ideas of the time.

Manilius sees the universe as the work of an all-powerful creator who has arranged the heavens and the celestial bodies so that they move and exercise their influences in a beautiful celestial pattern.

'This god, then, of whom I speak,' he writes, 'who is the all-controlling reason, gives the living creatures of earth an origin in the heavenly signs. Though these signs be far removed from us, yet does he so make their influence felt that they give to nations their life and their fate and to each man his own character.'[2]

Manilius also treats of astrological anatomy, which was later to become the basis for medieval 'astro-medicine'.

---

[1] Franz Cumont, *Astrology and Religion among the Greeks and Romans*, III.
[2] *Manil. Astr. II.* Tr. H. W. Garrod, 1.82.

'The Ram, chief of the signs, has for his special province the head; the beauty of the human neck falls within the arbitrament of the Bull; the two arms, with shoulders conjoined, are assigned in equal division to the Twins. The breast is placed under the Crab, the Lion holds sway over the sides and back. The loins come down to the Maid as her proper lot. The Balance governs the buttocks, the Scorpion has his glory in the genitals, the thighs are subject to the Centaur, Capricorn is lord of both the knees, the legs are the power of the Water-Carrier, and the Fishes claim for themselves the governance of the feet.'[1]

Manilius was not the only Roman poet to be inspired by astrology. Horace too shows himself to be versed in the subject when he asks himself whether he was born under Libra, Scorpio, 'the dangerous part of the horoscope', or Capricorn, 'tyrant of the sea of the Hesperides'.

> '*Seu Libra seu me Scorpios aspicit*
> *formidulosus pars violentior*
> *natalis horae, seu tyrannus*
> *Hesperiae Capricornus undae.*'

Astrology also had its detractors among Roman writers, one of whom was the satirist Juvenal. He was of the opinion that women were the chief cultivators of it.

'Avoid meeting with a lady', he says, 'who is always casting up her ephemerides, who is so good an astrologer that she has ceased to consult and is already beginning to be consulted; such a one on the inspection of the stars will refuse to accompany her husband to the army or to his native land.'[2]

The fact that astrology aroused so much controversy among Roman intellectuals is an indication of how strongly it was making itself felt. But astrology did not remain merely a source of inspiration for writers. Had it done so, its influence would never have attained the power that it did. Persuasive though

---

[1] Ibid, line 456.
[2] Flammarion, *History of the Heavens*, Tr. J. F. Blake.

they were, it was not men like Manilius who gave the art its essential power and vitality. The real explanation for this lay in the status held by astrology among the devotees of the various cults of oriental origin which flourished in Rome. The Phrygian cults of Cybele and Attis; the Syrian religion of Baal; the Persian creed of Mithraism; all were influenced to some degree by astrology.

A theory which featured prominently in these cults was that of 'catasterism' or 'translation to the stars', a belief which had played a significant part in Greek religion and mythology where heroes like Hercules, Perseus and Andromeda, Castor and Pollux, were thought to reside in the sky in the form of constellations. This theory came to Rome where it was applied to prominent men as well as to the heroes of myth.

According to one theory, the soul, being composed of the lightest substance of the universe, rose automatically upwards after death. It was purified by the elements as it ascended and finally found its peaceful resting-place in the uppermost zone. In some cults the soul required a god to lead it on its hazardous journey. Hermes was the name frequently applied to this deity in conformity with the Greek legend.

Another cult held that the soul had originally descended to earth through the planetary spheres, gaining from each one a different earthly quality. After death it had to reascend through the spheres, shedding these qualities and arriving at the outermost sphere in its pristine state of purity.

These oriental religions were particularly well adapted for the Roman Empire as it later developed. As the emperors became successively more dictatorial they became increasingly obsessed with their own divinity and naturally enough turned to the oriental priests for support. Loyal to the Egyptian and Syrian cults of the god-king, these priests gave the emperors a religious justification for their despotism.

The emperor became the image of the Sun on earth and was worshipped as god and master by right of birth (deus et dominus natus) who had come down from the heavens to rule as the Sun's regent. This cult of the Sun reached its peak under the emperor Elagabalus (Heliogabalus), whose obsession with his own divinity reached the point of insanity. But even the later Christian emperors, Constantine and Constantius, showed signs of paying homage to the Sun-god cult.

Astrology in Christianity and Neo-Platonism

So far I have not mentioned the most important of the eastern religions which existed in the Roman Empire and the one which was later to outshine all the others and finally dominate the entire Western world, namely Christianity. Like the other religions of the Graeco-Roman world, Christianity did not develop in isolation. It was not delivered to the world wrapped up in a neat doctrinal parcel but underwent a long process of formation, during which many different sects of Christianity struggled for supremacy and in which many different influences played a part.

At this time astrology was, as we have seen, an important ingredient in the intellectual and religious atmosphere of the Graeco-Roman world. Its symbolism and vocabulary were common currency, even among those who did not believe in its scientific validity. Thus any second-century theologian who sought, as certain Christian sects did, to fuse Christianity with current beliefs would have to take astrology into account. As it happened, the Christian sects which laid themselves open in an extreme way to alien influences were ultimately defeated by the more orthodox Christians. It would be wrong to exaggerate the influence of astrology on Christianity, but some very interesting facts emerge when we look at those sects which, although branded as heresies, continued to exercise their influence even after orthodox Christianity had been established.

In the first century AD there arose a group of Christian cults which are now loosely grouped together under the name of 'Gnosticism'. It is difficult to give a precise definition of this term, since there was wide divergence of doctrine between the various Gnostic sects. Nevertheless, it is possible to pick out certain fundamental beliefs which they had in common.

The word 'Gnosis' is a Greek term meaning 'knowledge', and the basic tenet upon which the Gnostic faith rested was that salvation depended not on faith or morality but on knowledge. The way to paradise was by knowing and acting upon the basic truths about man's relation to God and the cosmos. The different Gnostic sects varied in their ideas of these truths, but their theories were all based on a common theology and cosmology. Both of these, in their turn, were greatly influenced by the widespread astrological beliefs of the age.

The Gnostic religion, however, made an extraordinary reversal of the previous attitude to the planetary divinities. Whereas in Hermeticism and the other mystery cults which I have mentioned the planetary gods were revered as guardians of man's fate, in Gnosticism they were regarded as deadly enemies to be despised and struggled against.

In order to understand this, it is necessary to outline the basic beliefs of Gnostic theology and cosmology. The Gnostics conceived of a basic division between the divine world and the material world. The latter comprised the entire cosmos including the stars; the former was of a purely spiritual nature and lay far beyond the limits of the visible universe. What made Gnosticism particular anathema to orthodox Christians was that the Gnostics regarded the creator of the cosmos as an inferior god who had to be overcome if man was to return to his true father and creator, the alien god of the spiritual world. Under the inferior god, or demiurge, were ranged other subsidiary powers called Archons (rulers), each of which had his own sphere of influence in the material world.

Man, according to the Gnostics, is composed of two elements, one material and mundane, the other spiritual and extra-mundane. Both his body and his soul are part of the mundane portion, created by the demiurge. But enclosed within his soul is a non-terrestrial element, sometimes referred to as the spirit or 'pneuma' and sometimes as the 'spark'. This element, according to the Gnostics, is a portion of the divine substance from the outer world which has fallen into the material world and is being held there deliberately by the demiurge and his lackeys. The principal device created by the demiurge and the Archons for this purpose is man. By perpetuating himself, man is unconsciously perpetuating his imprisonment in the material world.

These beliefs are set within the familiar old cosmology of the spheres. Only now the spheres are a series of prisons surrounding the innermost dungeon which is the Earth. Each of the Archons is ruler of one of the seven spheres and their collective rule is known as *heimarmene*, universal fate, again an astrological concept. Each Archon attempts to bar the passage through his sphere of the souls who are trying after death to escape from the world and return to the supreme creator.

Here we have something very similar to the Roman cult which held that the soul must ascend through the elements after death before it can reach its final destination. One of the major differences, however, is that the agent whose function it is to guide the souls to their resting-place is not Hermes, but the abstract concept of knowledge. The attainment of this knowledge constitutes the most important step for the Gnostic, since, according to his theories, ignorance is an active force working against him and is part of the condition which has been imposed upon him by the Archons.

Let us look at some examples of these beliefs in the Gnostic scriptures. One of the most famous of these is the *Pistis Sophia*,[1] a Coptic Gnostic text found in Upper Egypt and believed to have been written in the fifth century AD. The text consists of a conversation between Jesus and his disciples after his death and resurrection. Jesus has just returned to his disciples after ascending into heaven and is telling them of his experiences on the ascent.

He first describes the terror with which he inspired the Archons as he passed through their region:

> ' "And all the rulers and all those who are in the Fate, were thrown into agitation and fell on one another and were in exceeding great fear on seeing the great light that was about me . . .
>
> And Adamas, the great Tyrant, and all the tyrants in all the aeons began to fight in vain against the light . . .

[1] *Pistis Sophia.* Tr. G. R. S. Mead.

And I took from them a third of their power, that they should no more be active in their evil doings . . .

And the Fate and sphere over which they rule, I have changed and brought it to pass that they spend six months turned to the left and accomplish their influences and that six months they face to the right and accomplish their influences." '

What Jesus means by this last statement is that he has weakened the power of the *heimarmene*, or Fate, by introducing irregularity into the operations of the planets. He has not done away with their power altogether, but he has arranged it so that any caster of horoscopes will now have a greatly diminished chance of being accurate in his predictions.

Mary Magdalen, who is one of Jesus' audience, asks him whether astrology will continue to be effective since he has not taken away the power of the planets, but merely confused it.

' "My Lord, will not then the horoscope-casters and consulters from now on declare unto men what will come to pass for them?"

And Jesus answered and said unto Mary: "If the horoscope-casters find the Fate and the sphere turned towards the left, according to their first extension, their words will come to pass, and they will say what is to take place. But if they chance on the Fate or the sphere turned to the right, they are bound to say nothing true . . ." '

Further on in the text Jesus gives his disciples an elaboration of the way the planets and their influences were arranged by the creator.

' "He bound eighteen-hundred rulers in every aeon, and set three hundred and sixty over them (i.e. the 360 degrees of the zodiac), and he set five other great rulers as lords over the three hundred and sixty and over all the bound rulers, who in the world of mankind are called with these names: the first is called Kronos, the second Ares, the third Hermes, the fourth Aphrodite, the fifth Zeus." '

Further on, Jesus goes on to explain that the only planet exercising a good influence is Zeus (Jupiter). The creator arranged it this way because the planets 'needed a helm to steer the world and the aeons of the sphere, so that they might not wreck it [the world] in their wickedness'.

These illustrations show that although most of the Gnostics did not approve of astrology as a method of divination, they nevertheless recognised that it could be effective and their thinking was deeply imbued with astrological symbolism. Had their ideas prevailed over what became orthodox Christianity, the Christian religion would have had a very different history, and the influence of astrology on it would have taken a very different form. As it was, astrology did creep into Christianity in other ways as we shall see when we come to examine the progress of astrology in the Middle Ages.

Our examination of the Roman period would not be complete, however, without a mention of the movement known as neo-Platonism, which both rivalled and fertilised Christianity in its early development. The man generally regarded as its founder was Plotinus. He was born, of Greek blood, at Lycopolis in Egypt around AD 203. In about the year 244 he settled in Rome where he spent the rest of his life teaching and writing, and enjoyed the esteem of many influential men including the emperor Gallienus.

His views on astrology have been given different interpretations. Porphyry, for example, in his *Life of Plotinus*, says that the latter devoted much of his writing to the refutation of astrology, and the fourth-century astrologer Julius Firmicus Maternus regarded Plotinus as an enemy of astrology. If, however, we examine what Plotinus had to say about the subject, we find that he was not inimical to it. On the contrary, his criticisms are in the nature of suggestions for improving astrology and bringing it more into line with a Platonic view of the universe.

Like Plato, Plotinus believed that the stars were living beings. 'And with respect to the stars,' he wrote, 'both those which are in the inferior spheres and those which are in the highest orb, what reason can be assigned why they are not

Gods, since they are moved in order and revolve with such beautiful bodies?'[1]

In his *Ennead* he states that 'it is abundantly clear that the motions of the heavenly bodies affect things on earth, and not only in bodies but also the disposition of the soul'.[2]

Like many later Christian writers, however, Plotinus finds unpalatable the idea that all human actions are caused by sidereal phenomena and he attacks the Gnostics for believing that the planets and the spheres over which they rule exercise a terrible tyranny over men.

Thus Plotinus finds himself in a dilemma familiar to those who attempted to theorise about astrology. He recognises that the stars have an influence on human affairs yet he is unwilling to surrender freedom of will to them.

He resolves the dilemma by concluding that the stars and the affairs of men are both symptoms of a more fundamental pattern arising from the fact that the universe is a single being between whose parts there is relation of perfect harmony. Celestial movements, therefore, are signs rather than causes of the future. This is a doctrine which was used by many later theorists. Carl Jung, for instance, argued something very similar in his theory of 'synchronicity'.

Thus Plotinus removes one of the commonest objections to astrology and arrives at what was to be the general medieval Christian position regarding it. Plenty of room was allowed for astrological prediction while at the same time the Christian could rest confident that through the exercise of his will he could remain master of his fate.

---

[1] *Select Works of Plotinus*. Tr. T. Taylor. Ed. G. R. S. Mead, 1895.
[2] Lynn Thorndike, *History of Magic and Experimental Science*.

Chapter 4   Oriental astrology

Introduction

While the Western version of astrology was being practised by
the Greeks and Romans, different forms of the art were
developing in the orient, notably in India and China.

Although the origins of oriental astrology are difficult to
determine with any precision, it is probable that both Chinese
and Indian astrology were germinated by Mesopotamian ideas.
There was an outward movement of population from Mesopotamia which started in about the third millennium BC, and it
is thought that the migrants brought with them to India and
China such rudimentary astronomical concepts as that of the
360 degrees of the ecliptic.

Scholars have supported the theory of the Western origin of
Chinese civilisation by pointing to such evidence as the resemblance between cuneiform writing and Chinese script, and the
similarities between Chinese and Babylonian folklore. In the
case of India, they point to such mythological links as the reappearance in India of the Persian Sun-god Mithra as the
Indian Sun-god Mitra.

The link between Indian and Babylonian culture was the
invasion in the second millennium BC by foreign tribes who

had previously been in close contact with Babylonian knowledge.

After this initial impetus Chinese and Indian civilisation developed more or less independently of Western influence for many centuries. In China, one of the products of this civilisation was a complex and sophisticated astronomical-astrological system which for a long time formed an integral part of Chinese ethics and religion. India, which produced a less sophisticated astrological system than China, was also subjected to a larger number of alien influences. Nevertheless, Indian astrology too was highly individual in character.

The influence of the old systems is still to be discerned in modern Chinese and Indian astrology. It is therefore worth examining these systems in some detail.

Chinese astrology

It is impossible to understand the astronomy and astrology of ancient China without first knowing something of the philosophical and religious atmosphere in which they developed. It would be well to begin therefore by outlining some of the basic characteristics of the Chinese view of the cosmos.

Whereas the Greeks, for example, thought of the universe as a living, changeable organism, the Chinese tendency was to look upon it in a more mechanical way. The universe, as they saw it, was a vast Chinese box, constructed in a most meticulously logical fashion and containing many different compartments.

The Chinese had a strong propensity for looking at their environment in terms of numbers, and they liked to arrange their ideas into numerical groups. All the numbers up to twelve were associated with groups of concepts important to the Chinese mind. Thus, to take three as an example, there were three kinds of heavenly light—that of the Sun, Moon and stars; three sacrificial animals—the ox, the goat and the pig; and three kinds of abundance—good fortune, abundance of years, and abundance of sons.

At the centre of this numerical scheme of things was the

The Moon in Cancer; a page from an Arabic manuscript of a work by the ninth-century Baghdad astrologer, Albumasar

Titlepiece to a sixteenth-century German book of astrological prophecy. The two inner circles depict the planets and the signs. The outer circle shows the houses and the various aspects of life that they govern. For example, the second house, the house of riches, shows a man counting his money; the seventh, the house of marriage, shows a couple being wed

system based on two elementary units: the *Yang* and the *Yin*. Just as modern science sees the world as a series of complex configurations of atoms, so the Chinese saw it as a series of permutations of numbers of these two basic principles.

The *Yang* was associated with masculinity, brightness and motion; the *Yin*, with femininity, darkness and rest. The *Yang* and *Yin* were also associated with the Sun and Moon respectively. From the very earliest times, this system was regarded by the Chinese with the highest veneration, and those who understood it were thought to possess the key to all knowledge.

This orderly, numerical view of things was applied by the Chinese to the heavens as much as to any other part of their environment. They divided the sky into five regions or 'palaces'; these consisted of a central palace around the pole, and four equatorial palaces corresponding to the four seasons of the year. Like the Babylonians and the Greeks they had twelve signs, but these were based on a different scheme from that of Western astrology. The signs were not divisions of the sky but of the equator. Thus they were more like the houses of Western horoscopy. Each division of the equator corresponded to one of the twelve double-hours of the day as well as one of the twelve months of the year. The signs were ranged alternately under *Yin* and *Yang*, and bore the names of the following animals: tiger, hare, dragon, serpent, horse, sheep, monkey, hen, dog, pig, rat, ox.

The central concept of Chinese cosmology was that of revolution around a fixed centre, and it was on this formula that the Chinese based their astronomy, government and system of social laws. Thus, the emperor, around whose throne earthly matters revolved, was considered to be a copy of a celestial emperor whose throne was the pole star around which the heavens revolved. Confucius expressed this idea when he said: 'The sovereign who reigns by virtue is similar to the polar star. He stays immobile in the centre and everything regularly revolves round him.'[1]

[1] L. de Saussure, 'Le Systeme Astronomique des Chinois', *Archives des Sciences Physiques et Naturelles*, Vol. 1, 1919.

E

Originally there was a clear distinction between the celestial emperor and his residence the polar star. Later, however, th distinction faded and the emperor came to be identified wit the star. It was believed that if the earthly emperor were in efficient and failed to carry out his rites properly, the regularit of the seasons would change, the movements of the planet would become abnormal, and disaster would overtake empir and dynasty.

This correspondence between the earthly and celestia emperors was reflected in certain codes of behaviour. Fo example, in solemn audiences the emperor always faced sout (like the pole star), while his subjects faced north. 'To turn t the south' and 'to turn to the north' are expressions which throughout Chinese history, have meant 'to act as sovereig and 'to act as subject'. This idea was also reflected in th ceremony of ancestor worship, during which the head of th family faced north to worship the ancestors, and south to fac his family and servants.[1]

The number five is one which figures prominently in al Chinese thought. There were, as I have mentioned, five celes tial palaces. These corresponded to five earthly divisions con sisting of a central region and four cardinal regions. There wa also a theory of five elements, which was systematised by Tsou Yen (born between 350 and 270 BC). According to this theory the world was made up of five elements: wood, fire, earth metal and water. These elements were associated with the points of the compass and the seasons of the year. Earth wa linked with the centre point of the compass. Water, fire, wood and metal corresponded respectively to: north, south, east and west; and to winter, summer, spring and autumn. All change of nature were explained according to this quinary theory, and all phenomena—colours, flavours, notes of music—were adapted to it.

Furthermore, there was a belief that the succession of im perial dynasties was related to the interaction of the elements. As an illustration of this, Needham quotes the following passage attributed to Tsou Yen:

[1] Ibid.

'Each of the Five Virtues [Elements] is followed by the one it cannot conquer. The dynasty of Shun ruled by the virtue of Earth, the Hsia dynasty ruled by the virtue of Wood, the Shang dynasty ruled by the virtue of Metal, and the Chou dynasty ruled by the virtue of Fire.

When some new dynasty is going to arise, Heaven exhibits auspicious signs to the people. During the rise of Huang Ti [The Yellow Emperor] large earthworms and large ants appeared. He said, "This indicates that the element Earth is in the ascendant, so our colour must be yellow, and our affairs must be placed under the sign of Earth." '[1]

After this theory took hold, each dynasty practised rites and ceremonies appropriate to its particular element. The basis of the theory was the idea that each element was able to conquer another. Wood was able to conquer earth, because, when in the shape of a spade, wood can dig up and make shapes of earth. Metal could conquer wood by cutting it. Fire could conquer metal by melting it. Water could conquer fire by extinguishing it. Finally, completing the cycle, earth could conquer water by damming it up and constraining it.

The five planets also had a place in the quinary system, each one being associated with a particular colour, element, sense, and so on. Needham sets out the correspondences as follows:[2]

Elements	Heavenly bodies	Planets	Colours
Wood	stars	Jupiter	green
Fire	Sun	Mars	red
Earth	Earth	Saturn	yellow
Metal	*hsiu* constellations	Venus	white
Water	Moon	Mercury	black

[1] J. Needham, *Science and Civilisation in China*, Vol. 2, Ch. 13.
[2] Ibid.

Domestic animals	Viscera	Sense organs	Emotions
sheep	spleen	eye	anger
fowl	lungs	tongue	joy
ox	heart	mouth	desire
dog	kidney	nose	sorrow
pig	liver	ear	fear

Gradually, a custom developed of naming the planets by their ruling elements, so that one often spoke of 'wood' instead of 'Jupiter'. In addition to these elemental associations, each planet had a different significance depending on whether it appeared nearest to the point of rising of the Sun or of the Moon. This governed whether the planet was linked with *Yang* or *Yin*. The various names given to the planets under these different forms are set out in the following table given by Knappich.[1]

Planet	Element	Under Yang (Sun)	Under Yin (Moon)
Jupiter	wood	1. *chia*	2. *yi*
Mars	fire	3. *ping*	4. *ting*
Saturn	earth	5. *wu*	6. *chi*
Venus	metal	7. *keng*	8. *hsin*
Mercury	water	9. *jen*	10. *kwei*

The positive, *Yang* aspect of a planet signifies the corresponding element in its adaptable, man-modified state; the negative, *Yin* aspect signifies the element in its raw, natural state. Looking at the above table, we see that Jupiter, or wood, is known as *chia* in its *Yang* aspect and *yi* in its *Yin* aspect. *Chia* is wood in its hard, adaptable form, that is the form it takes when used as a building material. In this form it has an affinity for hard metal (*keng*), but an antipathy towards flowing water (*kwei*). The other aspect of Jupiter, *yi*, is wood in its original, living, green state. In this form it fears hard metal, but loves flowing water.

These different planetary forms constitute a kind of second

[1] W. Knappich, *Geschichte der Astrologie*.

stem of signs. Thus, in addition to the twelve zodiacal signs, the Chinese also had ten planetary signs—five under *Yang* and five under *Yin*. When a horoscope was cast, both of these sets of signs, with all their corresponding significations, were taken into account, and a highly complex and detailed picture of the native was built up.

The other elements in the Chinese horoscope were the sixty double-signs and the twenty-eight lunar mansions. The double signs were formed by permutations of the five positive planetary signs with the six zodiacal *Yang* signs; and of the five negative planetary signs with the six zodiacal *Yin* signs. The lunar mansions corresponded to the days of the lunar month and were ranged under the twelve signs—so many mansions to each sign. I shall discuss the system of lunar mansions more fully in the section on Indian astrology.

Some interesting comparisons can be made between Chinese and Babylonian astrology. Carl von Bezold, for example, compares extracts from a Chinese book called the *Shih Chi* (Historical Record), written in about 100 BC, with similar ones from Babylonian cuneiform texts.[1] The following comparisons are quoted by Needham from Bezold's text.

(a) Cuneiform: If Mars, after it has retrograded, enters Scorpio, the King should not be negligent of his watch. On so unlucky a day he should not venture outside his palace.

    Shih Chi: If (the) fire (planet) (Mars) forces its way into the *hsiu* Chio then there will be fighting. If it is in the *hsiu* Fang or the *hsiu* Hsin this will be hateful to kings.

(b) Cuneiform: If Mars is in (name of constellation missing) to the left of Venus, there will be devastation in Akkad.

    Shih Chi: When Ying-Huo (Mars) follows Thai-Pai (Venus) the army will be alarmed and despondent. When Mars separates altogether from Venus, the army will retreat.

C. von Bezold, *Sze-ma Ts'ien und die Babylonische Astrologie*.

> (c) Cuneiform: If Mars stands in the house of the Moon
> (and there is an eclipse), the King will die,
> and his country will become small.
>
> *Shih Chi:*   If the Moon is eclipsed near Ta-Chio this
> will bring hateful consequences to the
> Dispenser of Destinies (the Ruler).
>
> (d) Cuneiform: If the Northern Fish (Mercury) comes near
> the Great Dog (Venus), the King will be
> mighty and his enemies will be over-
> whelmed.
>
> *Shih Chi:*   When Mercury appears in company with
> Venus to the east, and when they are both
> red and shoot forth rays, then foreign king-
> doms will be vanquished, and the soldiers of
> China will be victorious.

Another ancient Chinese document, the *Ku Wei Shu*, of un-
certain date, also contains passages reminiscent of the reports
by the Babylonian priest-astronomers to the king. Needham
quotes the following as an example:

> 'The Thien Chieh [Heavenly Street] lies between the *hsiu*
> Mao [Pleiades] and the *hsiu* Piu [Hyades]. The sun, the moon,
> and the five planets go in and out [by this street of heaven].
> If Ying-Hui [Mars] stays in this street, and does not go
> through it, then the whole world will be in danger [of
> disorder].
>
> The Chuan Shih [Hanging Tongue, ie the six stars in
> Perseus] governs rumours. If Ying-Huo stands near by it
> there will be rebellions among the people, the prince will be
> injured "by rumours and robbers will arise".'[1]

Needham is of the opinion that Chinese prediction was based
on similar principles to those used by the Babylonians, and that
it was these principles, rather than specific astrological knowledge, that passed from Babylonia to China.[2] The development
of the individual horoscope did not appear in China until the
first century AD.

[1] Needham, *Science and Civilisation in China*, Vol. II, Ch. 14.
[2] Ibid.

Indian astrology

Nothing approaching the modern system of horoscope astrology appeared in India until around the fourth century BC when the Greek influence began to penetrate the country. Long before this, however, the Indians had shown a preoccupation with the stars which showed traces of their contact with Babylonian astrology through the Aryan tribes.

According to the Hindus, the original source of religious wisdom was to be found in the seven ancient sages known as the *Rishis*. The word *Rishi* is derived from a similar word meaning 'to shine'. The original *Rishis* were the seven stars, or shiners, of the constellation Ursa Major which was revered by the Aryans. It was by the *Rishis* that the sacred hymns known as Vedas were supposed to have been revealed. These texts, which to this day are regarded with the greatest reverence, are thought by modern scholars to have been composed in about 1000 BC.

One of them, the *Rig Veda*, is quoted by the modern Indian writer G. V. Raghava Rau in support of his theory that the early Hindus were familiar with the divisions of the zodiac. One of the most interesting passages which he quotes is the following: 'Twelve are the fellies; and the wheel is single; three are the naves. What man hath understood it? Therein are set together spokes three hundred and sixty which in no wise can be loosened.' The number 12 in this passage, coupled with that of 360, certainly savours strongly of astrological numerology and seems to indicate that the authors of the Vedas were familiar with the fundamentals of Mesopotamian astrology.

In early Hindu folklore, we also find a concept very similar to the Greek idea of catasterism. Alberuni, whom I shall come to later, quotes an ancient text known as the *Vishnu-Dharma* which contains the following statement: 'Those who by their pious deeds have obtained a place in the height sit there on their thrones, and, when shining, they are reckoned among the stars.'[1]

One of the earliest complex astrological concepts to emerge

[1] *Alberuni's India*, Ch. 50.

in India was that of the lunar mansions or *Nakshatras*. Although the Indians probably did not invent these, they can take the credit for developing them to a higher degree of sophistication than any other nation. In this system, the ecliptic is divided into twenty-eight parts, each corresponding to a day of the lunar month, and each possessing a special significance. Alberuni wrote:

> 'The Hindus use the lunar stations exactly in the same way as the zodiacal signs. . . . The astrologers attribute to each station a special nature, the quality of foreboding events, and other particular characteristic traits, in the same way as they attribute them to the zodiacal signs.'[1]

Today, the Indian astrologers use the lunar and solar zodiacs in conjunction, but in the early days there seems to have been some opposition between the advocates of the two systems. Brennand, in his *Hindu Astronomy*, suggests that these two zodiacs were the origin of the names of two of the ancient races of Indian princes known as 'The Children of the Sun' and 'The Children of the Moon'.

It is not only in the Vedas that the influence of astrology on early Hindu thought is shown. Another ancient series of texts which demonstrate the influence is the *Institutes of Manu*. These are of much later origin than the Vedas. They were composed in Sanskrit and were supposed to have originated from Manu, the son of Brahma, the supreme godhead of Hinduism. Their purpose was to teach certain religious and civil duties to the inhabitants of the Earth. The Brahmin, for example, is urged to perform periodic sacrifices in honour of the lunar mansions. Here are some examples from the advice given to Brahmins in the *Institutes of Manu*:

> 'On the days of conjunction and opposition let him [the father of a family] constantly make those oblations which are hallowed by Gayatri, and those which avert misfortune; but on the eighth and ninth lunar days of the three dark fortnights at the end of Agrahayan [an old name for one of the

1 Ibid.

lunar mansions] let him always do reverence to the Manes of Ancestors.

In the month of Ashvin let him cast away the food of sages, which he before had laid up, and his vesture, then become old, and his herbs and roots, the sun in the sign of Canya [the Virgin], must be shunned.

Having daily performed the Upakarma [domestic ceremony with sacred fire] at the full moon of Sravana or of Bhadra, let the Brahmin fully exert his intellectual powers and read Vedas during four months and one fortnight.'[1]

One of the earliest instances of anything approaching modern horoscope astrology occurs in connection with Dasaratha, a mythical Indian prince renowned for his study of astronomy, whose son Rama was supposed to have been born in about 961 BC. When Rama attained the age of manhood, Dasaratha decided to hand over some of his legal responsibilities to his son because of certain celestial signs.

'My star, O Rama, is crowded with portentous planets— the Sun, the Moon's ascending node, and Mars. Today the Moon rose in Punarvasu [one of the lunar mansions], the astronomers announce her entering Pushya tomorrow; be thou installed in Pushya. The Sun's ingress into Pushya being now come, the Lagna of Karkata [the sign of Cancer, in which Rama was born] having begun to ascend above the horizon, the Moon forbore to shine; the Sun disappeared, while it was day, a cloud of locusts, Mars, Jupiter, and other planets inauspicious approaching.'[2]

Although such instances show the presence of rudimentary horoscope astrology as early as the tenth century BC, it was not until many centuries later that Indian astrology reached anything like its present degree of sophistication. The real flourishing of Indian astrology began in about AD 300 under the influence of Hellenistic ideas.

It was at this time that the series of early astronomical

[1] W. Brennand, *Hindu Astronomy.*
[2] Ibid.

writings were composed in which the bulk of Hindu astronomy is set down. The best known of these is the *Surya
Siddhanta*. Although the works contain little astrology, in the
modern sense of the word, the *Surya Siddhanta* does devote a
chapter to the interpretations of celestial movements.

This era also produced Vahara Mihira, a man who today is
one of the most revered arbiters in matters of Indian astrology.
He lived in the sixth century AD and practised at the court of
King Vikramaditya. Like Ptolemy, he summarised all the
astronomical and astrological knowledge of his time.

Under the influence of Greek astrology and mythology, the
Indian gods were widely adapted to those of the Greek pantheon, and the days of the week were named after the planets.
The twelve signs of the Indian zodiac are also mostly transla-
tions of the Greek signs, and their characteristics and properties
were borrowed from the Greek tradition. The system of the
houses also entered, under Hellenic influence, into Hindu
astrology. Following the Western pattern, the houses were
related to the affairs of everyday life. The first house governed
the native's body; the second his material possessions; the
third his relatives; the fourth his dwelling, and so on.

But in addition to these Greek elements there were a number
of concepts which were purely Indian. One of these was the
doctrine of *Karma* and reincarnation which became one of the
fundamental teachings of Hindu astrology. The *Karma* is the
factor which determines the progress of the soul through its
various incarnations. According to Knappich, *Karma* appears
in the following three aspects: first, as *Sanchita*, the sum or
result of acts committed in the previous incarnation; secondly,
as *Prarabda*, acts of the present incarnation which are subject
both to the influence of the previous life and to the exercise of
free will in the present one; thirdly, as *Agami*, future, unrealised
acts. Thus the progress of the soul from one incarnation to
another is conditioned by a mixture of free will, *Karma* and
fate. Astrology was widely used by the Hindus to determine
what stage a man's soul had reached.

One of the fullest accounts of the practice of astrology in
India is to be found in a book by the eleventh-century Persian

traveller Alberuni, who entered India with the Muslim armies. Alberuni was a distinguished astrologer in his own right and his main work *The Elements of Astrology* is admired to this day. *Alberuni's India* contains a detailed examination of Hindu astrology. Although himself a Muslim, Alberuni is careful to treat the Hindu beliefs with respect, and writes of their practices with great understanding.

One interesting observation which he makes is on the relation between the zodiacal signs and parts of the body. According to him, the correspondences are as follows:

Aries	head
Taurus	face
Gemini	shoulders and hands
Cancer	breast
Leo	belly
Virgo	hip
Libra	under the navel
Scorpio	male and female genitals
Sagittarius	loins
Capricorn	knees
Aquarius	calves
Pisces	feet

It is interesting to note that many of these correspondences agree with those given by Manilius which I mentioned in Chapter 3—for example the relation between Cancer and the breast, Scorpio and the genitals, Capricorn and the knees. This is another indication of the influence of Greek astrology.

The characteristics of the planets as given by Alberuni are also similar to those of Greek astrology. Jupiter, Venus and the Moon are lucky, whereas Saturn and Mars are unlucky. Mercury is variable, depending on the planet with which it is combined. A striking exception however, according to Alberuni, is the Sun, which was considered by the Hindus to be an unlucky planet.

He also describes the way in which the Hindus attributed each month of pregnancy to the rule of a particular planet. Venus supposedly governs the first month, in which the semen and the menstrual blood become mixed; Mars, the second month, in which the embryo attains consistency; Jupiter, the third, in which the limbs begin to branch off; the Moon, the fifth, in which the skin appears; Saturn, the sixth, when the hair grows; Mercury, the seventh, in which the child becomes complete and receives its memory. The eighth month is the crucial one because it is then that the embryo becomes particularly susceptible to the substances of food which it absorbs for the first time. This month is therefore not under the influence of a particular planet, but merely any influences in the horoscope which might cause or prevent miscarriage. The ninth month is governed by the Moon, and the tenth, if any, by the Sun.

After Alberuni's time, Indian astrology came increasingly under Western influences, the Greek infiltrations having been superseded by Muslim. Modern Indian astrology, however, still retains such individual features as the lunar mansions and the concept of *Karma*.

Astrology and early Christianity

As we have seen, the influence of astrology on Christianity is
displayed at its most striking in the beliefs of the Gnostics. But
the disappearance of the Gnostics did not mean that astrology
ceased to influence the Christian religion. Although astrological concepts were not a central factor in orthodox Christianity as they were in Gnosticism, they nonetheless crept into
the doctrines of a number of Church writers. The Church itself
vacillated between tolerance and violent opposition to the art,
and the influence of astrology on Christianity was seen in a
number of different phases.

The first phase is represented by a number of astrologically
coloured Christian works which emerged from the welter of
neo-Platonic and other mystical creeds which were still flourishing in Rome when Christianity was adopted there. The most
interesting of these works is the strange collection of writings
known as the *Clementine Recognitions*. Although ascribed to
Clement of Rome, they were not written by him and their
authorship and date of origin are unknown. Nevertheless they
had a great influence on many Christian writers and are frequently quoted. In the writings, astrology figures prominently.

The *Recognitions* are ostensibly a series of accounts written by

Clement to James, the brother of the Lord, describing certain happenings and discussions in which he (Clement) and the apostle Peter had taken part not long after the death of Christ. Another character who figures in the accounts is the sorcerer, Simon Magus, who is also mentioned in the New Testament. Narrative about the doings of these different characters is interspersed in the writings with long doctrinal and philosophical passages.

In the latter, astrology is treated with respect. In the first book there is a passage which explains that God created the celestial bodies in order that 'they might be for an indication of things past, present and future', and that these signs, although seen by everyone, are 'understood only by the learned and intelligent'.[1] Further on it is stated that Abraham, 'being an astrologer, was able from the account and order of the stars to recognise the Creator'.[2]

A long discussion about astrology takes place when Peter Clement and Clement's father are gathered together debating various religious matters. They begin by considering whether the perpetrator of an evil action can be blamed for his deed if the deed was fated.

Clement asks his father whether it is true that, according to him, certain evils are produced by malignant planets like Saturn and Mars, and good things by beneficent ones like Jupiter and Venus. The father, who is evidently a believer in astrology, replies that this is so. Clement then asserts that a crime such as adultery is no less blameworthy because it has been caused by evil planets. The father objects to this argument and asks how, if a person's genesis compels him to sin, he can be blamed for sinning.

They continue to argue in this vein and finally reach a compromise. It is concluded that, however strong the influence of the planets, there always remains freedom of the individual will, entailing responsibility for action. Clement sums it up as follows:

[1] *The Recognitions of Clement*. Tr. Rev. T. Smith. In the Ante-Nicene Christian Library, Vol. III, I, 29.
[2] Ibid, I, 32.

'A mathematician [ie an astrologer] can indeed indicate the desire which a malignant power produces; but whether the acting or the issue of this desire shall be fulfilled or not, no one can know before the accomplishment of the thing, because it depends upon freedom of will.'[1]

It was not only through esoteric works like the *Recognitions* that astrology penetrated Christian thought. Many prominent early Christian thinkers were either firm believers or were sympathetic towards the art.

One man who combined astrological erudition with a firm belief in Christianity was Julius Firmicus Maternus who lived during the reign of Constantine. He was greatly respected as an astrologer and his name crops up frequently throughout the Middle Ages in discourses about astrology. His main work on the subject was the *Mathesis*, composed some time between AD 334 and 337. In it he sets out to reconcile astrology with Christianity and in attempting to do this, reaches the same compromise that we found in the *Recognitions*, namely the conclusion that although the heavenly bodies influence men's lives, this influence can always be resisted by a sufficient exercise of the will.

Another prominent Christian believer in astrology was Synesius who lived from about AD 370 to 430 and was made a bishop in the Christian Church. He spoke of comets as harbingers of disaster and held that astrology prepared men for the more exalted mysteries of theology.

Such men were, however, exceptional cases. They ran counter to the general trend of Christianity which was against astrology. As the religion jelled into orthodoxy, it became increasingly violent in its attacks on all creeds with pagan associations. Astrology came into this category. Another thing which made its beliefs unpopular was the implication contained in them that the stars were arbiters of human destiny—a theory that was anathema to most Christians.

The attack against astrology was led by Augustine (AD 354 to 430) whose opposition to it had all the bitterness of the

[1] Ibid, X, 12.

convert. He says in his *Confessions* that he was at first attracted to astrology, and only when the case of dissimilar twins was put to him did he decide that astrology was vain. From then on he was a sworn enemy of the sidereal art. His case against it, which is summed up in his *De Civitate Dei*, is weakened by the fact that, in his eagerness to demolish astrology, he uses arguments which contradict one another. He is unable to make up his mind whether he is against astrology because it is erroneous or because it is a form of evil magic. In the end he tries to have it both ways and adduces the absurd argument that astrology is vain, but that where its predictions are true this is due to the intervention of demons.

Although Augustine's arguments were weak, the weight of his influence and the opposition of the Church in general contributed to the suppression of astrology. Another factor which worked to its detriment was the widespread decline of learning which took place during the early Middle Ages. Even in its popular manifestations, astrology requires a modicum of literacy to survive and this was lacking in the early medieval centuries. Thus astrology disappeared almost completely from the European scene and was not to regain its former glory until the twelfth century.

Astrology's preservation in the Arab world

Meanwhile, however, across the Mediterranean, another great civilisation was coming into flower—that of the Arab world with its great centres of learning at cities like Baghdad and Alexandria. While astrology languished in Europe, it was kept alive in the Muslim world and it was from here that it was later to return, reinvigorated, to Europe.

Astrology is thought to have made its first significant appearance in the Muslim world in the eighth century AD when the Caliph Al-Mansur of Baghdad founded a school of astrology in the city with the help of a Jew, Jacob ben Tarik. In due course this school became a renowned centre of astrological learning.

Astrology, as it developed in the Arab world under the guidance of Muslim and Jewish scholars, presents an interest-

Above The horoscope, etched on rock-crystal, of the German soldier and statesman, Albrecht von Wallenstein (1583–1664)

Left Portrait of an unknown astrologer by the seventeenth century Dutch artist Cornelius Bega

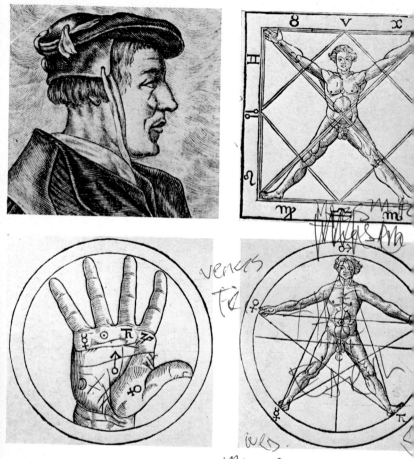

Top left The German magician and astrologer Cornelius Agrippa (approx. 1486–1536), and some engravings illustrating his discussions of palmistry and of man as a microcosm. These and the portrait are from a seventeenth-century English edition of his *de Occulta Philosophia*

ing contrast with the classical astrology of the Roman and Greek worlds. In classical astrology, predictions about the future had played an important part; in the Arab version, they are of minor importance. The Arabs were preoccupied mainly with the two branches of the science which were termed in Latin *interrogationes* and *electiones*. The former were a series of rules which enabled the astrologer to help in the catching of a thief, the recovery of lost possessions and other matters of a similar nature; the latter enabled him to determine the best moments for carrying out the tasks of everyday life, from major ones like beginning a journey, to comparatively trivial ones like cutting one's fingernails.[1]

By no means all the astrologers of the Arab world were Muslims or Jews. One of them, Thebit ben Corat, was a member of a small religious community, the Sabians, who were centred at Harran in Mesopotamia where Thebit was born in about AD 836. The Sabians denied the existence of God and based their religion entirely on the worship of the stars and planets, to which they made regular prayers and sacrifices. They were also interested in the relation of planets to metals and believed that each sign governed a different part of the body.

They were influenced in their beliefs by both Babylonian and Egyptian astrology and their religion seems to go back a long way. In *The Golden Bough* Frazer describes them as follows:

'The heathen of Harran offered to the sun, moon and planets human victims who were chosen on the ground of their supposed resemblance to the heavenly bodies to which they were sacrificed; for example, the priests, clothed in red and smeared with blood, offered a red-haired, red-cheeked man to "the red planet Mars" in a temple which was painted red and draped with red hangings.'[2]

In spite of the rather barbaric history of the Sabians, Thebit en Corat prided himself on being a member of their com-

T. O. Wedel, 'The Medieval Attitude Toward Astrology, Particularly England', *Yale Studies in English*, LX, 1920, Ch. 4.
Sir J. G. Frazer, *The Golden Bough*, Ch. 47.

F

munity. He was, however, forced to leave Harran because of a doctrinal disagreement. Moving to Baghdad, he set up a Sabian community of his own and became one of the Caliph's astronomers.

As a writer, Thebit had considerable influence on Christian Europe through his treatise on images which was twice translated into Latin. In it he declares that a knowledge of astrology is very helpful in performing acts of magic. By constructing astrological 'images', he says, it is possible to carry out by magic such feats as the driving away of scorpions or the recovery of stolen objects.[1]

The most renowned of the Arab astrologers was Albumasar, who practised in Baghdad at about the same time as Thebit and died around the year 886. He wrote extensively on astrology and many of his works were translated into Latin. The best known and most influential of these was his *Introductiorum in Astronomiam*, to use the Latin translation of its title. The book contains an interesting defence of Albumasar's art which greatly contributed to the reinstatement of astrology in Christendom. I owe the following summary of his argument to Professor Wedel.[2]

Albumasar begins by repeating Aristotle's theory that the heavenly bodies are composed not of any of the four elements of this world but of a 'fifth essence' which, unlike the earthly substances, does not suffer decay and dissolution. Furthermore, the stars move in a circular motion, the only one which is perfect and eternal. This circular motion is reflected in the earthly phenomena of growth and decay which are caused by the everlasting circular motion of the stars. Albumasar also follows Aristotle in drawing a distinction between the influence of the stars and that of the planets. The former governs the earthly phenomena which are either permanent or undergo gradual change; the latter governs the rapidly changing details of earthly life.

Coming to the perennial question of fatalism, Albumasar first makes a distinction between 'necessary' and 'contingent

[1] Lynn Thorndike, *History of Magic and Experimental Science*, Ch. 28.
[2] T. O. Wedel, *Medieval Attitude Toward Astrology*, Ch. 4.

actions. Necessary actions are those which always follow inevitably from given conditions; contingent actions are those which are governed by incalculable factors and are therefore debatable.

Man, says Albumasar, is made up of a reasoning soul and a physical body over which the soul rules. The stars, which are similarly constituted, are able to create harmony in the relation between the two elements in man: the physical, necessary element; and the spiritual, incalculable element. Thus the stars influence contingent as well as necessary acts.

In this way, Albumasar reaches his particular solution to the problem of free will. His arguments paved the way for later writers like Thomas Aquinas to complete the reconciliation between Christianity and astrology.

The return of astrology

Having glanced at astrology as it developed in the Arab world, we now return to Europe, where after several centuries of neglect of astrology the ground was being prepared for its return to prominence.

Already in the eleventh century a new spirit of humanism and enlightened enquiry was growing up in France under the inspiration of the school of Chartres. Astrology did not pass unnoticed by the students of the school. One of them, William of Conches (1080–1154), in his treatise *De Philosophia Mundi*, shows the influence of Julius Firmicus Maternus, whose name he couples with that of Ptolemy. Another writer of this period, Bernard Silvestris, was the author of a work, partly in verse and partly in prose, which deals with the creation of man. Neo-Platonic astrology figures prominently in it and there are long panegyrics of the glories of the stars.

It was into this atmosphere of enquiry that the first Arabian astrological treatises arrived early in the twelfth century. The man who pioneered their introduction into Europe was Adelard of Bath. He was born in England around the year 1100 and developed a strong interest in the middle eastern world to which he made a journey as far as Syria. On his return he devoted great effort to bringing Arab astronomy and geometry before the Latin world. He also wrote a number of books on his own account, one of which, the *De Eodem et Diverso*, contains a description of astrology as one of the seven virgins representing the seven liberal arts. 'If a man acquire this science of astronomy', writes Adelard, 'he will obtain knowledge, not only of the present condition of the world, but of the past and future as well. For the beings of the superior world, endowed with divine souls, are the principle and cause of the inferior world here below.'[1]

Another translator of Arabic works was Hermann of Dalmatia, a student of the school of Chartres. He was one of the translators of Albumasar's *Introductiorum in Astronomian*, one of the first of the Arabic astrological works to arrive in Europe.

It was thanks to the efforts of these and other scholars that by the middle of the twelfth century most of the major Arabic works on astrology were circulating in Latin translation. One thing which helped to make them acceptable to Christianity was their frequent use of Aristotelian cosmology. By this time Aristotle was regarded by many as the ultimate authority in all intellectual and philosophical matters. It was not difficult for the Christian to accept his doctrine that changes in the lower world were derived from heavenly motions that were in turn bestowed by a Prime Mover. All this was easily fitted into the Christian concept of the universe.

Nevertheless, the reconciliation between Christianity and astrology did not come about without a struggle and the exercise of a great deal of ingenuity. It took a scholar like Thomas Aquinas to work out the final formula of compromise. Aquinas got round the problem of free will by the usual device of asserting that, although the stars had an influence on human affairs, the will was still sovereign. The stars, he held, governed the bodily appetites and desires, which condition most human affairs since few can resist them. Thus the astrologer is capable of correct predictions about the great mass of humanity. His predictions cannot, however, include those few men who are able to rise above their appetites by the exercise of their will.

[1] Ibid.

Such concessions towards astrology on the part of men like Aquinas removed the fierce opposition which Christianity had formerly shown. For the next few centuries the two were to exist together in reasonable harmony.

The extent to which astrology had become accepted by the end of the twelfth century is shown by the following interesting event. The year 1186 was singled out by the astrologers as being the time when a conjunction of planets in the sign of Libra was to take place—a phenomenon that was thought to augur fearful disaster. Because Libra was an 'air' sign, it was thought that terrible wind-storms would be one of the many baneful results of the conjunction. It was predicted that cities in sandy regions were doomed; Egypt and Ethiopia were to become uninhabitable. In some countries earthquakes would take place and wreak equally dreadful destruction. The consternation caused by these predictions was widespread, and in some countries it was reported that people were building underground caves and holding special services to avert the disaster.

As it happened, very little occurred in the year 1186 to justify these fears, although some people thought that the astrologers were proved partially right by Saladin's victories in the Holy Land in the following year.

This embarrassment did not prove a set-back to the astrologers. Having firmly re-established itself by the end of the twelfth century, astrology consolidated its position and increased its following in the thirteenth. The schools in Mohammedan Spain remained the centre of European astrological learning; but outside Spain, Italy was the country where the science of the stars flourished most. From the thirteenth to the early sixteenth century there were chairs of astrology at many of the great Italian universities, including those of Bologna, Padua and Milan.

One of the most famous astrologers of the thirteenth century was Guido Bonatti, whose treatise, the *Liber Astronomicus*, was one of the most popular astrological works of the period. He leans heavily on the writings of the Arab astrologers as well as those of Ptolemy and the writers of the classical period.

His work was circulated in translation throughout Europe a~~n~~ as late as 1676 an English translation was made by the astrol~~o~~ger William Lilly.

An ironic recognition of Bonatti's fame is accorded him ~~by~~ Dante. A passage in the *Inferno* pictures a group of people wh~~o~~ are condemned for ever to look backwards with turned hea~~ds~~ as a punishment for having tried to probe the future durin~~g~~ their lives. Virgil points out one of these to Dante with th~~e~~ words 'Vedi Guido Bonatti . . .'[1]

For a time Bonatti was employed by the nobleman Cou~~nt~~ Guido de Montefeltro, who evidently found the astrologer~~'s~~ services extremely useful in aiding his military expedition~~s.~~ The story goes that Bonatti would direct the beginning of ~~an~~ expedition by striking on a bell, having first examined t~~he~~ positions of the stars. At the first stroke of the bell, the Cou~~nt~~ and his men would don their armour, at the second mou~~nt~~ their horses, and at the third gallop away.'[2]

In spite of Dante's condemnation of Bonatti in the *Infern~~o~~* there is much in his work that points to a preoccupation wit~~h~~ astrological symbolism and indicates a general belief in celesti~~al~~ influence. In the *Purgatorio*, for example, the spirit Marc~~o~~ Lombardo, although he denies that the stars are responsible f~~or~~ every cause, nevertheless admits that 'The heavens set you~~r~~ impulses in motion' (*Lo cielo i vostri movimenti inizia*).

It is in the *Paradiso* that the influence on Dante of astrologic~~al~~ symbolism is most clearly shown. Dante follows the usu~~al~~ cosmological practice of setting out the heavens in a numbe~~r~~ of different concentric divisions—in this case nine. Th~~e~~ *Paradiso* describes how Dante, accompanied by Beatric~~e,~~ ascends from the Earth through the heavens ruled respectivel~~y~~ by the Moon, Mercury, Venus, the Sun, Mars, Jupiter, Satur~~n~~ and the constellation of Gemini. Finally the ninth heaven is th~~e~~ invisible world beyond the stars. Having traversed these nin~~e~~ heavens, the poet reaches the final Empyrean Heaven, th~~e~~ abode of God and the angels and of departed souls. These nin~~e~~ divisions of the heavens correspond to nine degrees of ran~~k~~

[1] *Inferno*, XX, 118.
[2] T. O. Wedel, *The Medieval Attitude Toward Astrology*, Ch. 6.

into which the souls are grouped according to the virtue of their lives on earth. As the poet ascends, the souls come down to meet him at the stage appropriate to their station.

Here again we see a reappearance of the old Roman eschatological astrology already echoed in a different way by the Gnostics.

Although the Church was by this time very tolerant towards astrology it was still capable of striking down astrologers who went too far, as was proved by the case of Cecco d'Ascoli who was condemned to the stake by the Inquisition at Florence in 1327. D'Ascoli was professor of astrology at the University of Bologna and the author of, among other things, a long poem on astrological themes entitled 'l'Acerba'. One of the charges brought against him was that this poem was an impious parody of Dante's *Divine Comedy*, a charge for which there seems to be no foundation other than that d'Ascoli imitated Dante's style out of admiration. He was also accused of a number of other offences one of which was having taught that, by means of astrological spells, certain evil spirits could be controlled and made to perform magical feats.

D'Ascoli's execution was an extremely unusual event for this period. For the most part, astrologers were able to carry on their art unmolested and without fear of recrimination. Three centuries were to elapse before the discoveries of Galileo brought forward a new threat to astrology in the form of scientific scepticism.

Chapter 6   From the Renaissance to the Age of Enlightenment

Astrology in the Renaissance

The beginning of the Renaissance in Italy marks the zenith of astrology. Over the medieval centuries the science of the stars had emerged from its eclipse in the early Christian era to thrive in the fifteenth and sixteenth centuries as it had never done before. The intellectual climate of the Renaissance was particularly favourable to astrology. The revival of interest in the literature of ancient Greece and Rome drew the attention of educated men of the period to the works of Ptolemy, Manilius, Firmicus Maternus and the other ancient astrological writers. Furthermore the art of the Renaissance found great inspiration in classical mythology, much of which, as we have seen, has astrological associations. On a more popular level, the coming of printing in the middle of the fifteenth century made written prognostications and astrological writings more widely available.

Kings, popes, generals, physicians—all made use of the services of the astrologer. The ubiquitous figure with the astrolabe was to be found in all the great households of Italy where parents had the horoscopes of their children cast as a matter of course. A book on the period[1] contains a reproduc-

[1] J. Burckhardt, *The Civilisation of the Renaissance in Italy*.

on of a painting in the style of Giorgione depicting a mother nd father playing with a boy while to one side a bearded figure usies himself with astrological instruments drawing up the hild's nativity.

One of the key figures in the Renaissance was Cosimo de Medici, self-appointed dictator of Florence. Fortunately he was levoted not only to power but also to literature and the arts. He patronised artists, harboured Greek refugees from Constantinople, opened a public library, and collected many Greek and Latin manuscripts. One of his protégés was a young scholar named Marsilio Ficino (1433–1499), a student of medicine and philosophy. Ficino translated for Cosimo not only the works of Plato but also certain Hermetic treatises which he grouped together under the title of *Pimander*. These were full of Hermetic astrological lore and came to be widely read among students of the occult sciences. Ficino himself was a firm believer in astrology. In his medical treatise, *Liber de Vita*, he takes for granted that different parts of the body are related to different signs and that each planet has a different physical effect. Saturn he believed to be the planet of old age. Therefore, if one wished to remain young one must, he counselled, avoid objects with Saturnian associations and concentrate on those associated with the youthful forces of the Sun, Venus and Jupiter.

Another practitioner of astrological medicine was Philippus Bombast von Hohenheim, known to the world as Paracelsus (1493–1541). He was born in Switzerland, took a medical degree in Italy, and for a brief period taught medicine at the University of Basel. But his violent, vitriolic temperament brought him too many enemies to allow him to stay in one place for very long, and he spent most of his life travelling round Europe and writing feverishly.

Astrology played a strong part in his thinking. In one of his works, *Das Buch Paragranum*, he wrote:

'The inner stars of man are, in their properties, kind, and nature, by their course and position, like his outer stars, and different only in form and material. For as regards their nature, it is the same in the ether and in the microcosm,

man. . . . Just as the sun shines through a glass—as thoug
divested of body and substance—so the stars penetrate on
another in the body. . . . For the sun and moon and a
planets, as well as the stars and the whole chaos, are i
man. . . . The body attracts heaven . . . and this takes place i
accordance with the great divine order.'[1]

In another work, *De Peste,* he wrote:
'The art of astronomy helps us to discover the secrets of th
innate disposition of the heart and makes manifest the goo
and evil qualities with which nature has endowed man.'[2]

He did not, however, believe that the influence of the star
was irresistible. In another work he said that: 'The stars ar
subject to the philosopher, they must follow him, and not h
them. Only the man who is still animal is governed, mastered
compelled, and driven by the stars. . . .'[3]

The field of medicine was a fertile one for astrology, an
many other treatises on the subject of 'iatro-mathematics' o
astrological medicine were composed at this period. One of th
best known was Jean Ganivet's *Amicus Medicorum* (1431) whic
continued in use for two centuries afterwards. Like Ficino, th
author shows how maladies can be cured by relating the ail
ment to its astrological cause, and also how a person can avoi
illness by guarding against the weaknesses shown in hi
horoscope.

In 1437 there arose at the University of Paris a controvers
as to what days were most favourable for blood-letting. Th
arbitrators in the dispute recommended that every physicia
and surgeon should have an astrolabe 'in order to select fo
every day, every hour, and for fractions of the hours, a
ascendent sign corresponding to the sign in which the Moo
is found'.[4]

Some remarkable discoveries were effected through th
belief in a correspondence between the stars and the workin

[1] *Paracelsus, Selected Writings.* Ed. J. Jacobi. Part I.
[2] Ibid, Part III.
[3] Ibid, Part III.
[4] Lynn Thorndike, *History of Magic and Experimental Science,* Vol. IV
Ch. 44.

of the body. For example, Torella, physician to Pope Alexander VI and to his nephew, Cesare Borgia, explained syphilis as due to the conjunction of the four great planets in Scorpio which had taken place in 1484. He wrongly predicted that it would disappear in 1584 when a different conjunction would occur. These astrological deliberations did, however, result in the discovery of an early effective antidote to the disease, the application of quicksliver iodide, discovered in the attempt to counteract the noxious influence of the malefic planets by the use of a 'mercurial' substance.[1]

Other diseases such as influenza (literally a stellar 'influence') were also attributed to the effect of planetary forces and Guy de Chauliac, 'the father of surgery', attributed the great plague which swept Europe in 1345 to the influence of the conjunction of Saturn, Mars and Jupiter in Aquarius, observed on 24th March of that year.

Comets were one of the types of celestial phenomena which aroused the greatest interest and were thought by the astrologers to be of special significance for royalty. The papacy, too, was thought to be under the influence of comets, for one which appeared in 1472 caused the astrologer Perre le Lorrain to predict the death of Pope Paul II. For this act Lorrain was imprisoned and told that he would be put to death if his prediction proved false. On the afternoon of the supposedly fatal day his Holiness was still in good health and the astrologer's friends visited him in prison to warn him. He told them to await the hour, and sure enough the Pope died before the end of the day. Lorrain was then released from prison and heaped with honours.[2]

Other popes, however, were not so ill-disposed towards astrology. Pope Julius II had the day for his coronation and the day for his return from Bologna fixed by the astrologers and Pope Paul III was reported never to have held a consistory until the stargazers had fixed the hour.

Outside Italy, one of the courts where astrology flourished most was that of France, particularly at the time of Catherine

[1] Robert Eisler, *The Royal Art of Astrology.*
[2] Lynn Thorndike, *History of Magic and Experimental Science.*

de Medicis. Catherine was a member of the Florentine Medici family and was married at the age of fourteen to the Dauphin, later Henry II of France. When, after many years, she had failed to produce any children she began to consult astrologers, magicians and Tarot experts in the hope of curing her supposed sterility. In 1544 she gave birth to her first son and, convinced that this success was due to her magicians, her faith in the occult sciences was strengthened. She began to gather round her a large retinue of astrologers, most of them Florentines like Gabriel Simeoni, Cosme Ruggieri and Luca Gaurico. The last-named had already made quite a reputation for himself in Italy by correctly predicting that Alessandro Farnese would become Pope Paul III. As a reward, the Pope had knighted him and made him a bishop. Gaurico had also predicted that Giulio de Medici would have many political difficulties and beget great progeny. Sure enough Giulio, when he became Pope Clement VII, quarrelled with Henry VIII of England and fathered twenty-nine bastards.

The most famous of the astrologers employed by Catherine was not, however, a Florentine, but a Christianised French Jew. His name was Michel de Notre Dame, or Nostradamus as he is more commonly known. This austere and brilliant man had begun his career as professor of medicine and won great admiration by his work during a severe plague which swept through Marseilles in 1546. Early in life he had become aware of an uncanny gift he possessed for predicting future events and in addition had developed a taste for astrology with which he became increasingly preoccupied. In 1555 he published *Centuries*, a book of oblique predictions written in the form of quatrains. One of these predicted the death of King Henry II. It ran:

> *Le lyon jeune le vieux surmontera*
> *En champ bellique par singulier duelle:*
> *Dans cage d'or les yeux lui crevera*
> *Deux classes une, puis mourir, mort cruelle.*

(The young lion shall overcome the old on the field of battle in single combat. He will pierce his eyes in a cage of gold. This is the first of two blows, then he dies a cruel death.)

The year after the publication of *Centuries* Nostradamus was called to the French court and was shown high favour by the King and Queen who had him cast the horoscopes of their children. The Queen became obsessed with his prediction of her husband's death and insisted on his taking the most elaborate precautions.

But despite the Queen's precautions, Nostradamus's prediction was fulfilled to the letter. On July 1st, 1559, a tournament was held at which the King competed in a joust with the Compte de Montgommeri. The count's lance pierced the King's visor and a splinter gave him a fatal wound above the right eye. After ten days of terrible agony, he died.

The use of the word 'lion' in the prophecy has been explained by the fact that both the King and the count wore a lion emblem in the joust. The 'cage of gold' was of course the King's gilt visor. The blow was 'the first of two' that would destroy the House of Valois, for the King's son, Henry III, was assassinated by stabbing and the crown passed to Henry of Navarre.

From the time of her husband's death, Catherine became increasingly subservient to the dictates of her astrologers. When, for example, Ruggieri warned her to 'beware of St. Germain', she left the Palace of the Louvre which lay in the parish of St. Germain, ordered the building of the Hotel de Soissons with the inclusion of an astronomical observatory, and took up residence there.

In the end, however, this precaution did not succeed, if we are to judge from the circumstances surrounding Catherine's death on January 15th, 1589. Having been ill for some time and sensing that she was going to die, she drew up her will and asked for a priest so that she could give her final confession. A priest was sent and when the confession had been given, she asked the man his name. The priest replied that it was Julien de Saint Germain. 'Ah, my God, I am dead!' cried Catherine, remembering Ruggieri's warning; and later that evening she died.[1]

Before leaving the subject of astrology in France at this time,

Eugene Defrance, *Catherine de Medicis, Ses Astrologues et ses Magiciens-Envouteurs.*

it is interesting to remark that Catherine's contemporary, t
poet Pierre de Ronsard was also greatly drawn to the art of t
stars as many of his works testify. To quote only one examp
in his *Hymne des Astres* he wrote:

> 'Les Estoilles adonc se firent dames
> De tous les corps humains, et non pas de noz ames.
> Prenant l'Occasion a leur service, a fin
> D'executer ca-bas l'arrest de leur destin.
> Depuis, tous les oiseaux qui volent et qui chantent,
> Tous les poissons muets qui les ondes frequent,
> Et tous les animaux, soit des champs, soit des bois,
> Soit des monts caverneux, furent serfs de leurs lois:
> Mais l'homme par-sur tout eut sa vie sujette
> Aux destins que le Ciel par les Astres luy jette,
> L'homme, qui le premier comprendre les osa
> Et tels noms qu'il voulut au Ciel leur imposa.'

The beginnings of modern astrology

The middle of the sixteenth century saw the beginning of a
astronomical revolution that was soon to overturn the who
of medieval cosmology and widen the gap between astronom
and astrology. The event which marked the start of this rev
lution was the publication, in 1543, of the work by the Poli
cleric and astronomer Copernicus (1473–1543) entitled *I
Revolutionibus Orbium Coelestium*. This book revived the theor
propounded many hundreds of years earlier by Aristarchu
that the Earth moved round the Sun and not vice-vers
Copernicus did not, however, get as far as discovering th
elliptical shape of the planetary orbits, believing the circle i
be the symbol of perfection and the only shape possible for th
orbit of a planet.

The work begun by Copernicus was carried on by the Dan
Tycho Brahe (1546–1601), and his German pupil, Kepler (157:
1630). It was the latter who discovered the elliptical orbits
the planets. Another pioneer astronomer of this period wa
Galileo (1564–1642), who gave his support to the heliocentr

heory of Copernicus. He was aided in his observations by the
elescope which he perfected after its invention in Holland.
This instrument revealed, among other things, that the Milky
Way was composed of a vast number of stars and that Jupiter
had satellites which moved around the planet in accordance
with certain laws discovered by Kepler. Galileo's discoveries
soon brought him into conflict with the religious establishment,
and the story of his trial and recantation is well known.

The attitude of these astronomers towards astrology is interesting. Tycho Brahe practised it extensively and cast several
horoscopes for members of the Danish royal family. Kepler too
was addicted to the art and issued numerous predictions,
though it has been claimed that his motives in doing so were
purely financial. It is true that several times in his writings he
refers to astrology as the foolish daughter of astronomy. But
despite this degree of cynicism about astrology, Kepler retained
a firm belief in the validity of natal horoscopes. 'In general,' he
declared, 'there is no expedite and happy genesis, unless the
rays and qualities of the planets meet in apt, and geometric
agreement.'[1] Galileo was not drawn to astrology as strongly as
his two fellow astronomers and seems towards the end of his
life to have rejected it completely. Nevertheless he did study
the subject for a time and even drew up a number of nativities.

The revolutionary discoveries made by these men in the field
of astronomy were soon to render obsolete the medieval cosmology on which astrology was based. Nevertheless it was to
be some years before the full effect of the new astronomy was
felt and for a long time people continued to adhere to the old
cosmological theories. The symbolism of astrology continued
to appeal to many theologians because of the beauty of its
proportion and order. Religious writers of the sixteenth and
seventeenth centuries still talked of divine providence ruling
this world through celestial movements; of the division of the
universe into high, middle and low, corresponding to the
Trinity; of a series of celestial regions surmounted by the
Primum Mobile or Prime Mover.

A good example of a writer who used astrological ideas was

[1] *De Stella Nova*, Ch. 10.

Robert Burton (approx. 1576–1640), a clergyman and student of Christ Church, Oxford, who spent most of his reclusive life in the college reading esoteric subjects and writing his famous classic, *The Anatomy of Melancholy*. The book, which is a vast compendium of the ills and misfortunes of mankind and their remedies, owes a great deal to astrological typology, though Burton had reservations about the power of the stars over human lives. 'They lead, not drive,' he wrote, 'and so gently incline that a wise man will rule his stars: they rule us, but God rules them.'[1]

Burton is buried at Christ Church, and on his tomb is displayed his own horoscope (see illustration facing p. 94).

Another example of the continuing use of astrological symbolism is seen in the writing of the English poet and map-maker, John Norden, who set out his views on the nature and operating of the universe in a long and complicated poem entitled *Vicissitudo Rerum*.[2] His astrological terminology can be seen in the following extract from the poem:

> The first and greatest *Mover* of the rest,
> Imparts her moving to the lesser *Spheres*
> To men and beasts, and creatures as the *Test*,
> And tries the bodies that *Nature* upreares,
> Proving their temper, and their temper steres.
> Mong creatures that are earthly built,
> Best temper'd stand, distempr'd soonest spilt.
> Nay *Mindes* incline, and manners good and bad,
> Proceede (some say) by movings and aspects
> Of *Heavens* Spheres, and *Planets* wherewith clad,
> That give and take, and work the sole effects
> In *Men* and *Beasts*, and in all earthly sects:
> All which beginne and end by *influence*
> That doth proceed by *Heaven's* concurrence.

Norden's more illustrious contemporary, William Shakespeare, has also been claimed as a believer in celestial influence. Although it is tempting to try to justify this claim by seeking

[1] Op. cit., Part I, Sec. 2, Memb. 1, Subs. 4.
[2] Shakespeare Association Facsimilies, No. 4, 1931.

ut astrological references in his plays, I do not think that
hakespeare believed in the doctrines of astrology. It is true
iat he frequently refers to the influence of the stars, but a
loser examination of his work shows that for every reference
rhich supports the theory of stellar influence, there is another
rhich denies it. Here are two examples of such conflicting
:ferences. First, in *Henry VI*, Part III, Shakespeare makes
.ing Henry say:

> 'And that the people of this blessed land
> May not be punished with my thwarting stars,—
> Warwick, although my head still wears the crown,
> I here resign my government to thee.'

But on the other hand, in *Julius Caesar*, Cassius denies the
nfluence of the stars when he says:

> 'The fault, dear Brutus, is not in our stars
> But in ourselves, that we are underlings.'

Nowhere in Shakespeare's works do we find the sophisticated
strological symbolism of John Norden, or the panegyrics of
{onsard. All his references are simple statements about auspici-
)us or unlucky stars. If, in the works of a modern writer, we
:ame across the expression 'he was born under a lucky star' we
vould not immediately assume that the author believed in
:elestial influence, for the expression is common currency in
)ur language. Similar phrases were common currency in
;hakespeare's day and the use of them does not constitute a
)elief in the doctrines of astrology.

The period in which Shakespeare and Norden wrote was
:haracterised by two conflicting trends. On the one hand there
vas the great advance of learning and science typified by
Copernicus and Galileo, and on the other hand there was a
:eversion to the naive credulity of the Middle Ages, character-
sed by the wave of witch-hunting which broke out at the end
)f the fifteenth and continued into the seventeenth century.
Astrologers were often victims of this persecution. Neverthe-
ess, the power of medieval astrological symbolism can be seen

G

in its influence on the writings of the demonologists themselves. One of them, for example, Francesco Guazzo in his *Compendium Maleficarum*, says of another writer on the subject: 'Pierre Crespet has much to say concerning such imprisoned demons, namely, that in serving their masters some are saturnine, some jovial, some mercurial etc.'[1]

The attitude of royalty towards astrology at this time seems to have depended not on the accuracy of predictions, but on whether or not those predictions were favourable to the throne. For example, when the physician Senelles predicted from the horoscope of Louis XIII that the king would die in September 1631, he was condemned to the galleys and his property was confiscated. This did not prevent the next ruler, Louis XIV, from making use of the services of the astrologer Jean Baptiste Morin de Villefranche (*see* illustration facing p. 95). When the king married Anne of Austria, Morin was instructed to hide in the nuptial room at the consummation of the marriage and so cast the horoscope for the conception of the future dauphin.[2] Morin was, in fact, one of the most distinguished astrologers of his age as well as being a qualified doctor. His life's work was a treatise entitled *Astrologia Gallica* which took him thirty years to write and which did not appear until after his death.

Another monarch who was not averse to astrology was Elizabeth I of England who patronised the alchemist and astrologer John Dee. One of the services he performed was to fix the date of her coronation according to the astrological indications.

Some of the popes, as we have seen, were well disposed towards astrology, but others, like Urban VIII, condemned it strongly. Urban's condemnation may have been due to the adverse prediction of Father Morandi who calculated astrologically that the Pope would die in 1630. His prediction attracted attention, for a number of cardinals came to Rome expecting a conclave to elect a new Pope. The Pope, however, survived. Morandi was arrested and died a few months later of

---

[1] *Compendium Maleficarum*, 1608, Book I, Ch. 6.
[2] L-F. A. Maury, *La Magie et l'Astrologie dans l'Antiquite et au Moyen Age.*

a fever in prison. The following year Urban issued a bull against astrology.

Nevertheless it was a cleric who became the most famous astrologer of the seventeenth century. He was Placidus de Titis, a Benedictine monk and teacher of mathematics at several Italian universities. His main work was his *Physio-mathematica sive Coelestis Philosophia* in which he set out to meet the objections of an earlier opponent of astrology, Pico della Mirandola, who had argued that the celestial divisions on which astrology rested were abstract and unreal. One of the ways in which Placidus reconstructed the foundations of astrology was by reforming the house system so that the houses were no longer abstract geometrical divisions but stations in the Sun's daily journey around the Earth. His work was of such lasting value that he has become known as the father of modern astrology.

In England the controversy over astrology raged particularly strongly in the late sixteenth and early seventeenth centuries between supporters and defenders of 'judicial astrology', as the divinatory part of celestial science came to be known. One of the writers who took up their pens against it was Henry Howard, Earl of Northampton, who wrote *A Defensative Against the Poison of Supposed Prophecies*, published in 1583. One of the arguments he uses in the treatise is that astrological predictions are often the instrument of their own fulfilment.

> 'It chanced oftentimes that Pamphlets which prognosticated famine, have been the causes of the same, not by the malice of the Planets which are toyes, but by the greediness of the Husbandmen, who being put in fear of such a storm, partly by forestalment, and as often by the secret hoarding up of grain, enhaunce the prices in respect of scarcity.'

Like many opponents of astrology, Howard made the mistake of confining his discussion to the popular abuse of the art and ignoring its profounder aspects.

One of the most prominent of English astrologers was William Lilly whose prediction of the Great Fire of London is well known. Lilly was the son of an impoverished country

squire. Coming to London at the age of eighteen, he became a
domestic servant and later married his employer's widow.
This enabled him to pursue his education and take up the study
of astrology, at which he became extremely proficient. He soon
had a large clientele and was publishing almanacs under the
name of 'Merlinus Anglicus'.

A good deal of jealousy seems to have existed between rival
astrologers at this time, for Lilly's contemporary and former
pupil John Gadbury wrote as follows in his *Britain's Royal Star*
(1661):

> 'I know astrology is sufficiently under Hatches at this day
> in England, and by the major force of wise and ignorant,
> not only neglected, but condemned by reason of the Syco-
> phancy, Leidgerdemain, and Grand Jugling of that Arch-
> Parasite Merlinus Anglicus; who for many years hath been
> falsely reputed the Chief Astrologer among us.'

Astrologers were also subject to the political animosities
aroused by the Civil War. One of Lilly's bitterest professional
rivals was George Wharton, and the two were continually
swapping insults in their writings. The rivalry was aggravated
by the fact that Wharton was a royalist and Lilly a staunch
parliamentarian. When, however, Wharton was arrested for the
second time in 1649 for his royalist writings Lilly was prevailed
upon by their mutual friend Elias Ashmole to take pity on his
rival and intercede on his behalf with the authorities. After
Wharton was released he published an acknowledgement to
Lilly and henceforth the two remained firm friends.

Soon the tables had turned. With Charles II in power it was
Lilly who had become a political outcast. After the Great Fire
of London of 1666 he was suspected of having conspired with a
foreign power to cause the fire, partly because of some wood-
cuts that he published in 1651 depicting Gemini, London's
astrological sign, falling into flames. To answer the charge he
was summoned before a parliamentary committee investigating
the causes of the fire, but was acquitted after polite questioning.
His acquittal was partly thanks to his old friend Elias Ashmole
who had not forgotten his kindness to Wharton. Ashmole was

influential in government circles and did his best to prejudice the committee in Lilly's favour.

Ashmole was no less an interesting figure than Lilly. He was a remarkably versatile man—astrologer, alchemist, historian, herald, Fellow of the Royal Society, high-ranking civil servant and later founder of the Ashmolean Museum at Oxford. In his youth, astrology had been one of his great passions, and in spite of his other studies and important official duties he retained a keen interest in it throughout his life and always did his best to attend the Astrologers' Feasts that were held every year in London. Obsessed by the strong influence which he believed Mercury to exercise upon his character, he incorporated the symbol of the planet into his coat of arms.

Ashmole took his astrology seriously enough to believe that he could perform magical acts by harnessing the planetary forces through the use of talismans and sigils. It is reported that during a conjunction of Saturn and Mars he cast lead images in the shapes of caterpillars, flies, fleas and toads which he believed would afford protection against these pests. On another occasion he cast Martial and Venusian sigils in the shape of genital organs as a protection against the pox.[1]

Lilly and Ashmole were men of considerable intellect and, as such, were the exception in the world of astrology. The fact that, by this time, the best-known representatives of the art were mere commercial fortune-tellers is an indication that astrology was already going into decline.

The dark days of astrology

At the beginning of the eighteenth century astrology was made the object of a cruel jest by that arch-satirist Jonathan Swift. The victim was a man named Hewson, popular prognosticator and almanac-writer who traded under the name of 'Partridge' and who had frequently issued warnings to his readers to beware of impostors. In 1707 Swift decided to challenge this warning by publishing a bogus forecast entitled *Predictions for the year 1708, by Isaac Bickerstaff. Written to prevent the people of*

[1] C. H. Josten, *Elias Ashmole*, Vol. I, Ch. 3.

England from being further imposed on by vulgar Almanack Maker.
In this publication 'Bickerstaff' made a number of very precis
forecasts, one of which concerned the death of Partridge. '
have consulted the star of his nativity by my own rules', wrot
Bickerstaff, 'and find that he will infallibly die upon the 29t
of March [1708] next, about eleven at night, of a raging fever.

Partridge survived the fateful day without mishap. Imagin
his surprise, therefore, when soon afterwards Bickerstaff issue
another pamphlet entitled *An Account of the death of Mr. Par
ridge, the Almanack Maker, upon the 29th instant, in a letter from
Revenue Officer to a Person of Honour.*

Although Partridge published vigorous denials of his death
it was to no avail, for the joke was quickly taken up by othe
practical jokers. People would stop him in the street and as
him for money for the coffin and the funeral expenses. Th
Reader of his parish sent several messages asking him to com
and be buried decently. Worst of all, the Stationers' Company
who published his almanac, believed the announcement of hi
death and struck him off their rolls.

The unfortunate Partridge had to cease publishing hi
almanac and was not able to start up again until 1714 when h
published his *Merlinus Redivivus.*

This episode augured badly for astrology; already the tid
was beginning to turn against it. By the beginning of the
eighteenth century the whole intellectual climate of Europe
had changed. The Renaissance, the Reformation and the rise o
science had all contributed to the weakening of the Church's
authority in intellectual matters. Whereas before people had
taken the Church and Aristotle as the supreme arbiters i
academic questions, the men of the eighteenth century turne
to science and reason to answer the ever-increasing number o
questions which perplexed them. Soon the process of intellec
tual search became an end in itself and thinkers began to delight
in the gymnastics of abstract thinking for their own sake and
even recommended them as a healthy antidote to the foolish
illusions of religion and superstition. David Hume, for ex
ample, in *A Treatise of Human Nature*, recommended that men
should study philosophy so as to avoid being led into super-

stition by their instinctive desire to speculate about things outside the sphere of everyday life. He wrote:

'For as superstition arises naturally and easily from the popular opinions of mankind, it siezes more strongly on the mind, and is often able to disturb us in the conduct of our lives and actions. Philosophy on the contrary, if just, can present us only with mild and moderate sentiments; and if false and extravagant, its opinions are merely the objects of a cold and general speculation, and seldom go so far as to interrupt the course of our natural propensities.'[1]

Philosophers like Hume, Locke, Descartes and Berkely were not concerned with speculating about arcane or esoteric matters. They were concerned primarily with the process of thinking itself and the result of their labours was the forging of new intellectual tools.

This was the era which became known as the 'Age of Enlightenment'. The pendulum had swung to the opposite extreme from the religious dogmatism of the Middle Ages and now reason and common sense had become the cardinal virtues.

In such an atmosphere, astrology, like all other occult sciences, was naturally taboo. In the mania for 'enlightenment' which swept Europe, attempts were made in many countries to suppress astrology. Under such conditions it was not surprising that the art of astrology declined and its followers dwindled to a small number of ardent devotees. The result was that the hard core of remaining adherents to astrology went underground and studied their art in the lodges of the Freemasons, Rosicrucians and other secret societies which now came into full flourishing. In these societies, astrology and the other occult sciences were studied as symbolic systems of philosophy rather than as practical means of divination.

Few astrological books of any significance were written at this time, but a notable exception was a work by an Englishman Ebenezer Sibly. His book was called *The Science of Astrology or Complete Illustration of the Occult Science*. First published in 1790, it went through two further editions in 1812 and 1828. It con-

[1] Op. cit., Book I, Part 4, Section 7.

tained numerous horoscopes of kings, noblemen, statesmen and other prominent people. Sibly also wrote an astro-medical textbook *The Key to Physick and the Occult Science*. His brother Manoah, also an astrologer, translated two of the works of Placidus.

To make matters worse for the astrologers in this sceptical time, an event occurred in 1781 that struck a painful blow at the old astrological tradition. This was the discovery by Sir William Herschel of a new planet, which was at first called 'Herschel' and later 'Uranus'. The fact that there were now eight planets caused the number seven to lose a lot of its mystique and spoilt the symmetrical scheme of rulership of the signs. Later the astrologers were to be faced with the discovery of two more planets, Neptune and Pluto.

On the whole it was a bleak time for astrology. The scientist had rejected astrology in favour of the new astronomy begun by Copernicus, while the religious man had, for the time being, ceased to be interested in the mystical content of the ancient religious writings in which, as we have seen, astrology figured so prominently. The archaeologist and anthropologist had not yet appeared on the scene to stimulate a new respect for ancient beliefs and encourage a fresh interest in astrology.

The survival of astrology in Europe

Between its decline after its heyday in the sixteenth and seventeenth centuries and its re-emergence in England in the early nineteenth century, astrology was dormant. As I have mentioned, it was kept alive behind closed doors in the secret societies, and, to some extent, by occasional popular practitioners like the Sibly brothers. But with so few exponents, astrology had, for the time being, ceased to be a subject that interested the general public. What then was the background from which the new astrology of the nineteenth century emerged?

The answer to this question is that there were two separate backgrounds which already contained the germs of the modern division of astrologers into 'scientific' and 'occult' practitioners. First there was the background of experimental science; secondly there was that of occultism.

At the end of the eighteenth century, there emerged on the continent a number of writers interested in the border areas of science, such as Pasqually and Azais in France, and Mesmer in Germany. In the writings of these people astrology as such is hardly mentioned, but there is an interest in ideas similar to those of astrology, for example the ideas of man as a microcosm of the universe. Friedrich Anton Mesmer came very close to astrology when in 1776 he produced, as a thesis for a doctorate, a dissertation entitled *De Planetarum Influxu in Corpore Humano*.

This then was the experimental-scientific background. But more important at this time was the occult background. As long as there were students of the occult sciences there were those who believed, in a general sense, in celestial influences and were interested in the symbolism of astrology. An example was the English occultist Francis Barrett who, in 1801, published a book entitled *The Magus, or Celestial Intelligencer*. Little is known about Barrett except that on the title-page of the book he describes himself as a 'Professor of Chemistry, natural and occult philosophy, the Cabala etc. etc.'. He freely acknowledges in his preface that the book is mostly derived from other authors of whom he gives a strange and impressive list: 'Zoroaster, Hermes, Apollonius, Simon of the Temple, Trithemius, Agrippa, Porta (the Neapolitan), Dee, Paracelsus, Roger Bacon, and a great many others.'

Barrett describes himself as 'a warm advocate for stellar divination or astrology'. He echoes the microcosm theory when he says that 'we carry a heaven in ourselves from our beginning'. Evidently he had a certain amount of contempt for popular astrology, for in discussing free will (which he champions) he says:

'. . . our astrologers in most of their speculations seek without a light, for they conceive every thing may be known or read in the stars: if an odd silver spoon is but lost, the innocent stars are obliged to give an account of it; if an old maiden loses a favourite puppy, away she goes to an oracle of divination for information of the whelp. Oh! vile credulity, to think that those celestial bodies take cognizance of, and give in their configurations and aspects, continued information of the lowest and vilest transactions of dotards, the most trivial and frivolous questions that are pretended to be resolved by an inspection into the figure of the heavens.'

Barrett does not deal at all with conventional astrology and gives no instructions for the casting of horoscopes. Instead he describes the nature of the various planetary forces and tells how they can be harnessed by the use of talismans and charms.

A similar kind of symbolic astrology is set out in a much later French work, *L'Homme Rouge des Tuileries* by Paul Christian (pseudonym for Christian Pitois), published in 1863. The 'Red Man' of the title refers to the familiar spirit who was supposed to have advised Napoleon Bonaparte and been responsible for his victories. The Red Man also appears in a book by the clairvoyant Mlle Le Normand, called *Le Petit Homme Rouge des Tuileries*.

Christian's book is an intriguing and complex work. The text is in the form of a novel about an eccentric old man living in a dilapidated house in Paris and advertising himself as a '*Professeur des Mathematiques celestes*'. The old man possesses a manuscript which he claims to be 'fragments of a lost book' of secret wisdom. This manuscript, which is quoted in full, forms the bulk of the text, and in it the author explains his peculiar system of astrology.

Christian, like Barrett, echoes the pseudo-cabalistic astrology of Cornelius Agrippa and the other medieval occultists. The document tells us that: 'The seven spirits who have as their thrones the planets Saturn, Jupiter, Mars, the Sun, Venus, Mercury and the Moon, are the agents by which the universal Intelligence exercises its dominion over men and things.' The document goes on to explain that under these seven there are thirty-six inferior demons corresponding to the decans; these in turn rule over 360 intelligences which govern the degrees of the zodiac.

There follows a long exposition of Christian's astrological system, linking the planets and signs to the cabalistic angels and the keys of the Tarot. Basically the system is onomantic, that is to say it rests on the use of names as the basis of divination. A horoscope is worked out by using the letters of a person's name and the digits of the year in which he was born.

Apart from Christian, there were very few people in France who were interested in astrology *per se*. Occultists like Eliphas Levi and Papus professed a knowledge of it and mentioned it in their works, but it is clear from their references that astrology was incidental to their main interests.

Turning to Germany we find just as great a poverty of astrological teaching, though there are a few isolated examples. One of the earliest German astrologers of the nineteenth century was Julius Pfaff, a professor at Erlangen University. In 1816 he published *Astrology*, a book consisting largely of quotations from the works of famous astrologers through the ages. He also issued, in collaboration with his university colleague Schubert, a number of astrological textbooks, one of which was a condensed version of Ptolemy's *Tetrabiblos*.

Another nineteenth-century German writer on astrology was F. Nork whose *Die Ersten Elemente der Sterndeutekunst* was published at Leipzig in 1837. The system set out in this work is just as untraditional as that of Paul Christian. In his introduction, Nork writes of the annual cycle of nature being composed of two contrasting forces—one fruitful, the other destructive. These two forces correspond to the summer and winter months. Nork's discussion of the meaning of the astrological symbols is confined, as with Barrett and Christian, to the cabalistic and alchemical correspondences of the signs and planets. His system of calculation is a rather crude one and is based on a simple scheme of each of the planets ruling a different day of the week.

One of the few publications approaching an almanac to be issued in Germany in the nineteenth century was *The Horoscope of Napoleon III*, by Johannes Karl Vogt, published at Munich in 1860. As well as an analysis of the Emperor's horoscope, it contains a number of general predictions about the future of Europe and Germany.

This poverty of astrological writing throughout Europe made it difficult for any would-be practitioner of the science to find any rules to follow. Nevertheless, there were a few eccentrics who clung to astrology and developed their own individual versions of it. One of these was Lady Hester Lucy Stanhope (1776–1839), the niece of William Pitt and, for a time, his closest friend and confidante. After Pitt's death in 1806 she became dissatisfied with England, embarked for the Levant and, in 1814, settled in a fortress on the slopes of Mount Lebanon. By skilful intrigue she soon became a powerful gure in the area and came to be regarded with great superstion by the local people.

According to the *Memoirs of Lady Hester Stanhope*, as recorded y her doctor, Charles Lewis Meryon (London, 1845), Lady tanhope 'had a remarkable talent for divining characters by ae conformation of men'. The book also records how she xplained her system of astrology:

'A man's destiny may be considered as a graduated scale, of which the summit is the star that presided over his birth. In the next degree comes the good angel attached to that star; then the herb and the flower beneficial to his health and agreeable to his smell; then the mineral, then the tree, and such other things as contribute to his good; then the man himself.'

Speaking of her own astral spirit, Lady Stanhope said:

'I have a little angel under my command, the angel of my star—such a sweet little creature!—not like those foolish ones who are fiddling in Italian pictures. What fools painters are to think angels are made so!'

Many distinguished people came to visit Lady Stanhope at er mountain retreat. One of them was a German aristocrat oted for his erotic adventures, Prince Pückler Muskau. In a etter to the prince she waxed eloquent on astrology.

'A man born under a certain star will have, from nature, certain qualities, certain virtues and vices, certain talents, diseases, and tastes. All that education can do is merely artificial: leave him to himself, and he returns to his natural character and his original tastes.'

The Prince evidently shared her convictions, for he wrote to er: 'Like you, madam, I believe that astrology is not an empty cience, but a lost one.'

The Revival in England

England had been the country where astrology flourished most luring the sixteenth and seventeenth centuries. It was appro-

priate, therefore, that England should be the country to lea
the popular astrological revival that began in the early nin
teenth century.

One of the first nineteenth-century English works of con
ventional astrology (as opposed to the pseudo-cabalistic astr
logy of Barrett) was James Wilson's *A Complete Dictionary*
Astrology, published in 1819. This is a highly detailed textboo
adhering closely to the accepted astrological tradition an
leaning heavily on Ptolemy. 'The work of Ptolemy', the auth
states, 'is the only standard one we possess, and has served
a foundation for every other.'

A writer on a more popular level was John Worsdale wh
was known chiefly for his *Horoscope of Napoleon Bonaparte*. H
also published a book called *Astronomy and Elementary Phil*
sophy; Containing the Nativity of Princess Charlotte Augusta. In th
work he made great play with the dire consequences of th
conjunction of Saturn and Jupiter in Aries on June 19th, 182
As it turned out, very little untoward happened on that day.

That astrology was still legally regarded as an undesirabl
profession is shown by the case of Thomas White, a practisin
astrologer and author of *The Celestial Intelligencer; or, t*
Beauties of Science Investigated. White was arrested for makin
predictions to a client and died soon afterwards in Winchestc
prison.

A later prosecution, in 1865, is mentioned by Montagu
Summers in his *Witchcraft and Black Magic*. He quotes th
following extract from a Manchester newspaper of the sam
year:

'At the Sleaford Town Hall, yesterday, John Rhode
apparently a respectable man, living at 226 Regent Road, wa
charged, under the Vagrancy Act, with telling fortunes. A
girl named Ellen Cooper stated that she saw the prisoner a
his house on Tuesday. After she had told him the date of he
nativity, the prisoner cast her horoscope, and told her wha
she might expect would be her future fortune. For this sh
paid a shilling. . . . From information given by the girl
Cooper, two detective officers called at the prisoner's hous

on Thursday, where they found him with a female standing beside him whose future he was busy calculating, aided by an astrological work. . . . In the prisoner's house the officers found a large number of books, including "An Introduction to Astrology" by William Lilly; "Raphael's Prophetic Alphabet Almanack"; "Occult Philosophy" by Cornelius Agrippa (in manuscript); a work on horary astrology, etc. . . . In addition to these were manuscripts with forms of invocation to spirits to do the will and bidding of the invoker.'

We are not told what the penalty was, but it is safe to assume that it was at least a stiff fine. Clearly many people at this time still regarded astrology as akin to witchcraft.

A great leap forward in popular astrology was taken with the appearance of Robert Cross Smith (1795–1832) who became famous under the pseudonym of 'Raphael' and who was, in effect, the father of modern popular astrology. After being involved in a number of partially successful astrological publishing schemes, he launched, in 1827, a periodical called *The Prophetic Messenger*. This was an enormous success and is still published today under the title of *Raphael's Almanac, Prophetic Messenger and Weather Guide*. Raphael also wrote a number of books on astrology and fortune-telling in general.

He was helped by his influential friends, one of whom was the balloonist G. W. Graham. In 1822 he collaborated with the latter in producing a booklet on geomantic fortune-telling dedicated to Mlle le Normand. Raphael also knew William Blake and drew up the poet's horoscope.

Smith died in 1832 and was succeeded as Raphael by his pupil John Palmer, the first of a long line of successors to the title.

The second great figure in English nineteenth-century astrology was Lieutenant Richard James Morrison (1795–1874) who adopted the name 'Zadkiel'. Morrison entered the Navy as a young boy and retired on half-pay while still in his twenties. Soon after leaving the Navy he joined the Mercurii, a society started by Raphael. In about 1830 Morrison started up an annual publication called *The Herald of Astrology* by 'Zadkiel the Seer'. The title was changed a number of times and from 1848 onwards was known as *Zadkiel's Almanac*.

Unlike many astrologers, Zadkiel was a highly competent writer, and his wide reading enabled him to pepper his text with quotations and literary allusions. The style of *The Herald* is lively and entertaining. The 1831 edition contains a series of rather gloomy predictions for the following year, some of which are illustrated in its frontispiece (*see* illustration facing page 111). The style is appropriately portentous. For example part of the prediction for April runs:

'The gaunt and horrid spectre, DEATH, stalks through the land, and *many of the mighty, many of the low*, shall fall before his merciless scythe. Remarkable fluctuations in the funds will note this period.

The evil Mars is now in Aquarius. On the 7th he joins Herschel, in the 18th degree of that sign. The last time he passed Herschel in Aquarius was in April, 1830, when *King George the Fourth* was *seized with a fatal illness!* Affliction will again affect the *royal brow*. Some degree of illness may be apprehended; but *national trouble* will now indubitably add to his Majesty's sorrows.'

Among Morrison's books on astrology were *The Grammar of Astrology*, a small handbook that met with great success and was reprinted a number of times, and *An Introduction to Astrology*, a technical manual based largely on Lilly's *Christian Astrology* (1647).

Morrison was a colourful figure and an intelligent and widely educated man. He lived a curious double existence, keeping his life as Zadkiel separate from that of Lieutenant Morrison, R.N. Ret., the cultured man-about-town who was welcomed in the best society.

For many years Zadkiel's closest collaborator was a young London solicitor called Christopher Cooke, who helped in Zadkiel's lifelong, but unsuccessful, campaign to make astrology legally acceptable by amending the 1824 Vagrancy Act. Later Cooke became disenchanted with Morrison, partly because of the failure of certain business ventures which the two

The horoscope of Robert Burton, author of *The Anatomy of Melancholy*, on his tomb at Christ Church, Oxford

German woodcut of between 1520 and 1530, illustrating the idea that the sphere of the fixed stars was not the limit of the universe

Above The seventeenth-century French astrologer, Morin de Villefranche, who was employed by Louis XIV and whose *Astrologia Gallica* became a classic

Left Titlepiece to a German treatise on the 'Great Conjunction' of all seven planets in Pisces in 1524 which was

had launched and which Morrison had tried to run according to astrological indications. Cooke wrote two books on astrology: *A Plea for Urania*, 1854, and *Curiosities of Occult Literature*, 1863.

Another leading name of nineteenth-century astrology was William Joseph Simmonite, a Sheffield schoolmaster with a wide range of interests. He was a herbalist as well as an astrologer and in 1848 published a book called *Medical Botany or Herbal Guide to Health*. He was also a keen astro-meteorologist and for a time published an almanac, the *Meteorologist*. His most widely read astrological book was *W. J. Simmonite's Complete Arcana of Astral Philosophy*, to use the better known title of the second edition.

Another name I should mention in connection with this period is that of Alfred James Pearce (1840–1923) who became the third editor of *Zadkiel's Almanac*. Pearce originally intended to be a doctor, but was unable, for financial reasons, to take a medical degree. He did, however, practise as an unqualified assistant to other medical men for many years. At the age of twenty-one he joined Morrison's Astro-Meteorological Society, and in 1863, at the age of twenty-three, produced his first book: *A Defence and Exposition of the Principles of Astrology*. He also published a number of works on astro-meteorology. Pearce's best known book is his *The Text Book of Astrology* which was for many years a standard work for those learning astrology.

Less well known than Pearce in the field of astrology, though more distinguished in the academic world, was Richard Garnett (1835–1906), a member of the British Museum staff who became Keeper of Printed Books. He was a keen amateur astrologer and produced a cogent argument for his beliefs under the anagrammatical pseudonym of A. G. Trent. This appeared in the *University Magazine* of March 1880. One of his acquaintances was Samuel Butler whose horoscope he cast.

An important event in the history of astrology occurred a year after Morrison's death in 1874. This was the formation in New York by Madame Blavatsky and Colonel Olcott of the Theosophical Society. Theosophy, with its wide-ranging aims of encouraging the study of comparative religion and investi-

H

gating the unexplained laws of nature, played a large part in the revival of interest among intellectuals for subjects like astrology. Although Madame Blavatsky was not herself a great devotee of astrology, it is clear from her writings that she believed in its doctrines. In *The Secret Doctrine* she wrote that the sidereal motions

'are inseparably blended with the destinies of nations and men. . . . Ancient wisdom added to the cold shell of astronomy the vivifying elements of its soul and spirit—ASTROLOGY. In the prognostication of historical events, at any rate, there is no psychic phenomenon involved. It is neither *prevision* nor *prophecy* any more than the signalling of a comet or star several years before its appearance. It is simply knowledge and mathematically correct computations which enable the wise men of the East to foretell, for instance, that France is nearing such a point of her cycle, and Europe in general on the eve of a cataclysm, which her own cycle of racial *Karma* has led her to.'

Madame Blavatsky's successor, Annie Besant, was a more ardent disciple of astrology, and believed that it could be used as a guide in the education of children. In *A Study in Consciousness* she expressed the view that

'it is not the Star that imposes the temperament, but the temperament that fixes the epoch of birth under that Star. But herein lies the explanation of the correspondences Stars —Star-Angels, that is to say—and characters, and the usefulness for educational purposes of a skilfully and carefully drawn horoscope, as a guide to the personal temperament of a child.'

Under Annie Besant's leadership, the Theosophical Society became one of the leading sources of propaganda for the cause of astrology, and many prominent astrologers of the twentieth century were nurtured by it.

What theosophy helped to do was to make astrology more acceptable to the intellectual by bringing it into the context of a new kind of mental search—a search that involved the bringing together of many different religions, philosophies and beliefs.

The growth of popular astrology in Britain

At the turn of the century the biggest name in British astrology was that of Alan Leo (pseudonym for William Frederick Allen, 1860–1917). A former commercial traveller, he became interested in astrology in his twenties and was launched into the world of occultism by Walter Gorn Old, the astrological writer who later became famous as 'Sepharial'. Old introduced Leo to Madame Blavatsky, and from then on for the rest of his life Leo was a devoted member of the Theosophical movement. In 1890 he started *The Astrologer's Magazine* which later became *Modern Astrology*. He also set up a practice as an astrologer and, with the help of publicity from his magazine, was soon doing a roaring trade in mail-order horoscopes aided by a slave-driven staff of astrologers at his headquarters in Hampstead. He was twice prosecuted for fortune-telling. On the first occasion, in 1914, the summons was dismissed; but a second summons, in 1917, brought him a fine of five pounds with twenty-five pounds costs. Leo also wrote profusely on astrology. He was able to reach a wider public than his predecessors because he was the first British astrologer to write manuals of instruction for the layman. With the help of Leo's series of manuals *Astrology for All* it was possible for almost any dilettante to fancy himself an expert caster of horoscopes.

Leo's Friend Sepharial was a more prolific writer, though today he is less respected than Leo in the astrological world. He produced over forty books on astrology and for a time did a good trade in stock-market forecasts and astrological racing systems. He left the Theosophical Society when Annie Besant took over the European section after Madame Blavatsky's death.

In spite of the efforts of Leo, Sepharial and their immediate successors, astrology remained virtually unknown to the general public until 1930. In that year the *Sunday Express* discovered its sales potential and began to publish regular astrological features by R. H. Naylor. One of Naylor's earliest forecasts, a prediction of extreme danger to British aircraft, was proved unpleasantly accurate by the R-101 airship disaster soon afterwards. But such successes impressed his readers and so popular were his articles that other newspapers soon followed suit in employing astrological journalists. There was Edward Lyndoe in the *People*, Ann Maritza in the *Daily Mirror* and 'Archidamus' in the *Daily Mail*. Starting by publishing full-scale features, the newspapers soon discovered the demand for regular forecasts and were quick to develop the short astrological column that has since become so familiar.

By the time of the Second World War newspaper astrology had achieved a tremendous following. An article in the *New Statesman* of August 16th, 1941, reported that: 'Today more people follow their fate (or Hitler's) in the stars, as interpreted by the astrologers, than follow the day-to-day news of God (or Satan) as outlined by his archbishops and vicars.'

After the war the influence of astrology continued to grow. Today no mass-circulation popular journal can be without its astrological column, magazines like *Fate* and *Prediction* flourish, and every new year brings a spate of predictive almanacs.

All this is regarded with disdain by the high-brow astrologers who congregate at the Theosophical Society to listen to lectures on the finer points of their science. The Society is still the main promoter of the serious study of astrology in this country. The Astrological Lodge of the Society, founded in 1920 by Charles

O. Carter, issues a quarterly journal, *Astrology*, gives courses and awards diplomas.

There are some serious astrologers who, like Kepler, are prepared occasionally to work for the popular market, but generally there is a clear division between serious astrology and its foolish commercial daughter.

The revival in France

It was around the turn of the century that the countries of Europe other than Britain began to disinter the science that had been buried by the Age of Enlightenment. In France the renaissance of traditional astrology was pioneered by F.-Ch. Barlet (pseudonym for Albert Faucheux, 1838–1921). His *Traite d'Astrologie Judicaire*, 1895, was followed in 1897 by Fomalhaut's *Manuel d'Astrologie Spherique et Judicaire* which contains a remarkable anticipation of the discovery of Pluto thirty years later. 'There is a planet', wrote Fomalhaut, 'beyond the orbit of Neptune and its name is Pluto.' In 1902 appeared Henri Selva's *La Theorie des Determinations Astrologiques de Morin de Villefranche*, an edited version of Morin's great classic.

Ellic Howe points out in his *Urania's Children* that, whereas the British astrologers at this time were mostly professionals, nearly all their French counterparts had other jobs. Selva, for example, worked on the Paris stock exchange. Fomalhaut's alter ego was the Abbé Charles Nicoullaud, a Parisian parish priest. Another French astrologer, Paul Choisnard, was an artillery officer and a graduate of the Ecole Polytechnique.

The astrological movement in France grew steadily, and by the 1930s had achieved a mass market with the appearance of periodicals like *Votre Destin* (1935) and *Sous le Ciel* (1936).

The revival in Germany

The spectacular revival of astrology in Germany owed a great deal to the activities of the Theosophical Society whose German section had been founded in 1884. One of the leading figures in the revival was Hugo Vollrath, a sly opportunist who ran the Theosophical Publishing House at Leipzig under whose imprint most of the early twentieth-century Germa astrological literature was issued.

One of Vollrath's early ventures into the periodical field w the occult journal *Prana*, containing a monthly suppleme called *Astrologische Rundschau* and edited by the Austrian Ka Brandler-Pracht, one of the leading lights of the new Germa astrological movement. Brandler-Pracht had started his worl ing life as an actor, but had turned to astrology after attendin a spiritualist séance in Basle where he received a message fro the ether that he had a mission to serve the cause of astrolog After breaking with Vollrath in 1914 he moved to Switzerlan where he founded a number of astrological societies. He wa succeeded as editor of *Astrologische Rundschau* by Ernest Tied a man of racialist views whose astrological writings containe all sorts of Nordic propaganda.

It was not until after the First World War that astrolog became a subject of popular interest in Germany. When it di so this was largely thanks to the skill as a publicist of Fra Elsbeth Ebertin whose annual prophetic alamanac, *Ein Blic in die Zukunft*, was first published in 1917. Partly because c certain startling predictions about Hitler in the 1924 edition c the almanac, she soon became widely known and her service much in demand.

Other astrological periodicals followed suit. The movemer spread; astrological congresses were held; and attempts wer made to establish a national astrological organisation—some thing which neither Britain nor France had yet attempted. Th jealousy of rival astrological factions, however, prevented th latter scheme from coming to fruition, though a number o different organisations were established.

Astrology, which had started as a professional preserve, soo became a subject of interest for intellectuals with a penchant fo the occult, and in the years between the wars the scale of astro logical activity in Germany reached an unprecedented level.

During the war astrology in Germany suffered many set backs, the most disastrous being the purge of astrologers which followed Hess's flight to Scotland in May 1941. The officia explanation for this highly embarrassing event was that Hes had been insane and under the influence of astrologers. Astrology was therefore made the scapegoat; hundreds of astrologers were arrested and all astrological literature was banned.

After the war, however, it did not take long for the astrologers to come out of hiding. Their art revived and quickly regained its former following.

The United States

Astrology first appeared on the American scene in the late nineteenth century and was given great impetus by the formation of the Theosophical Society in 1875. The birth of the society started an avalanche of occultism in the United States. Thereafter there sprouted a profusion of 'Hermetic', 'Cabalistic' and 'Rosicrucian' societies, most of them interested, to a greater or lesser extent, in astrology.

One of the pioneers of astrology in America was a Dane called Max Heindel who had studied Theosophy under Rudolph Steiner in Berlin in the years 1901–3. After emigrating to the United States he joined a break-away section of the Theosophical Society called the Universal Brotherhood, and in 1909 founded his own organisation, the Rosicrucian Fellowship, centred near Los Angeles. He wrote many books on astrology, the most famous of which is his *Message of the Stars*.

Around the beginning of the century many other astrological societies with grandiose names came into being. There were, for instance: the First Temple and College of Astrology, the Esoteric School of Cosmic Science, and the Percy School of Chemistry of Life. Most of these schools are occult in character, but one, the Llewellyn College of Astrology, was founded with the intention of breaking away from the occult tradition. Llewellyn George, who founded the college at Los Angeles in 1908, professed a scientific type of astrology and had as his motto: 'facts not fancies'. In 1926 he founded the National Astrological Association which later became the American Federation of Astrologers and now has a headquarters in Washington. The Llewellyn College still continues and runs a highly successful publishing house.

It did not take long for the American astrologers to establish a position almost as influential as that of their Renaissance predecessors. Among the thousands of people who came to consult Evangeline Adams at her studio in New York in the 1920s were politicians, lawyers, financiers and government officials. One of her clients was the millionaire financier J. P. Morgan who paid Mrs. Adams in return for monthly astrological forecasts to help him in his financial speculations.

Today, popular astrology in America is big business and there are many consultant astrologers who derive enormous incomes from their clienteles. There are, as in Britain, a number of thriving mass-circulation astrological periodicals, and most of the big popular newspapers carry horoscope columns.

The Far East

Turning to the Orient we find that astrology has continued to prosper since ancient times without suffering from the fluctuating popularity experienced by European astrology. In certain countries, particularly India, it has attained the status of a highly revered science. Among the best-selling publications in India are the astrological almanacs called *panchaga* which are issued every year by learned astronomo-astrologers called *Jyotishi Pandits*. In the whole of India there are only about a dozen men qualified to hold this title. To attain it is a long process, calling for great perseverance. First the aspirant must study for twelve years at a Hindu university to become a qualified astrologer. Then, before he can 'put up his plate', he must serve nine years' apprenticeship with an experienced astrologer. Finally, he must spend another twenty to thirty years of work and research before he becomes qualified to draw up a *panchag*.

So respectable has astrology become in India that even the police are using it. I quote from a report in the *Daily Telegraph* of February 19th, 1968:

'The Stars as Sleuths

When the Indian police are thoroughly probing a possible crime they enlist astrologers as well as fingerprint and other experts, and they have now asked for a copy of the horoscope of Deendayal Upadhyaya, leader of the Hindu Nationalist Party, whose battered body was found a week ago on the railway near Varanasi (formerly Benares).

Party leaders allege that he was the victim of a political murder. The police want professional astrologers to see if his horoscope can throw light on the events leading to his death.

An unfavourable conjunction of the stars, however, may also indicate that he died by accident.'

In both India and Ceylon nearly all weddings are arranged by the astrologers. Not only does the astrologer decide whether or not the pair are well matched, but he also determines the day on which they should wed. If the celestial signs are particularly auspicious it is not uncommon, in a town of 10,000 people, to have 100 weddings in a single day.

Not only weddings are fixed by astrologers. When Burma was due to receive her independence the day for the ceremony was changed from January 6th, 1948, the day decided on by the British, to January 4th, the Sunday after the Moon's third quarter. This was considered by the astrologers to augur better for the country's future.

It is not surprising that when an adverse prediction is made widespread consternation and chaos result. Such an occasion was January 1962 when Indian astrologers were deeply disturbed by the impending conjunction of seven planets in Aquarius—a phenomenon which, according to them, heralded widespread calamity and possibly the end of the world. Food prices rose drastically as people stored up for the coming disaster; transport became impossible as thousands fled the country; the Prime Minister, Nehru, was guarded by hundreds of extra security men; and 250 priests in Delhi sat down for a twenty-one day session of incantations in a last-minute attempt to placate the heavenly powers. Evidently their prayers were successful, for no Armageddon occurred.

Certain other oriental countries have made attempts to prevent this kind of panic by stamping out astrology. In 1960, for example, the main Saigon newspapers announced that they were suspending their horoscope columns in an attempt to eradicate superstition among the Vietnamese people.

Opposition to Astrology

In Europe, too, there have been voices raised against astrology. In 1961 an issue of the Vatican weekly magazine *Osservatore della Domenica* contained an article by Fr. Reginaldo Francisco condemning astrology. 'If one really believes in the horoscope,' said Fr. Francisco, 'one commits a grave sin. One falls into heresy by denying free will and one violates the first commandment.' It would be interesting to know if, when he wrote this, Fr. Francisco was aware that the women's weekly magazine *Cosi*, edited and printed entirely by nuns, had been running a horoscope column regularly for years.

A similar indictment of astrology came from the Archbishop of York, Dr. Cyril Garbett, in his monthly diocesan letter issued on August 31st, 1934. The Archbishop criticised 'croakers and fatalists who can only see gloom and darkness in the years ahead'. He went on: 'I have sufficient faith in human intelligence to believe that those who study the predictions of astrologers do so for their own amusement and not out of any serious attempt to acquire information about their future.'

Such attacks as these have had little or no effect on the belief in astrology which has continued to grow to the mystification of the scientist and the consternation of the sceptic.

Chapter 9   Some aspects of modern astrology

Science versus occultism

We have seen how, in the nineteenth century, there were already signs of a split between those who had a scientific interest in astrology and those who held that it was a secret occult or 'Hermetic' art. One of the early twentieth-century exponents of the scientific view was the Frenchman, Paul Choisnard, who was the first to employ statistical methods in testing the validity of horoscopes. His most famous work is his *Langage Astrale* in which he attempts to justify astrology on scientific lines while at the same time not discarding the elements of the tradition. In his introduction to the 1928 edition of the book, he sums up the conflict between the two sides as follows:

> 'The occultists, on the one hand, are reluctant to admit that positive science is by itself capable of reconstituting a knowledge which they believe to be of a priestly nature—a knowledge to which they believe themselves to hold the key.
>
> The scientists, on the other hand, find it even more difficult to retract their scepticism and admit that "astrology is valid".
>
> This is why, in the two camps, there is a tendency to regard "ancient" astrology as being opposed to "modern" astro-

logy which the former cannot refute since it completely ignores the general precepts of the great fathers of astrology —Ptolemy, Thomas Aquinas, Kepler, and so on.

But these precepts are absolutely in accordance with the astrology which I have tried to reconstruct scientifically.'

Choisnard's attempts to justify astrology by statistical means were continued on a larger scale by the Swiss astrologer Karl Ernst Krafft, one of the victims of Hitler's purge. Krafft first became interested in astrology while a science student at Geneva University in the 1920s, and soon became fired with the ambition to make himself the apostle of a whole new theory of cosmic influences. For years he toiled at collecting birth-data, casting horoscopes and making statistical analyses. The final result of his work was a large and baffling book entitled *Traité d'Astro-Biologie*, published privately at Brussels in 1939. The methods used by Krafft have since proved of doubtful value, but his work did inspire others to attempt to put astrology on a scientific footing. The English astrologer, G. E. Sutcliffe, developed an 'electro-magnetic' theory of planetary forces; the French scientist, G. Lakhovsky, author of *Origine de la Vie*, had a theory that the planets send out waves that influence the human body; recently, the Nuremberg astronomer, Dr. Wilhelm Hartmann, has claimed that the traditional elements of astrology are derived from demonstrable physical relationships—a theory that he has set out in *Die Lösung des Uralten Rätsels um Mensch und Stern* (1950). Another recent researcher, M. Michel Gauquelin, has carried out extensive investigations into the whole question of cosmic influences. These I shall mention briefly in the final chapter.

In the occult camp, an outspoken critic of the scientific point of view is the French astrologer Alexandre Volguine. In his *Journal d'un Astrologue* (1957) he speaks of Choisnard and Gauquelin as follows:

'Their inherent fault is a distrust of esotericism, for true astrology has always been and will always remain a path towards esotericism. Whether one likes it or not, it is the open door to the sacred domain which transcends present-day science and where there is no place for statistics. It is the science of the soul, and the soul will always escape the scalpel of arithmetic.'

The view expressed in this passage is a common one, and would be shared by most astrologers of the 'theosophical' type. The occult side of astrology has wide ramifications, permeating Freemasonry, Rosicrucianism and other such fraternities. A passage in *The Meaning of Masonry* by W. L. Wilmshurst (1923) illustrates how some masons view astrology. The author explains that part of the purpose of the discipline of masonry is to enable the mason to build up 'an inner ethereal body which will form his clothing or covering, when his transitory outer body shall have passed away'. He goes on:

'Moreover, as in the outer heavens of nature the sun, moon and stars exist and function, so in the personal heavens of man there operate metaphysical forces inherent in himself and described by the same terms. In the make-up of each of us exists a psychic magnetic field of various forces, determining our individual temperaments and tendencies and influencing our future. To those forces also have been given the names of "sun", "moon" and planets, and the science of their interaction and outworking was the ancient science of astronomy, or, as it is now more often called astrology, which is one of the liberal arts and sciences recommended to the study of every mason and the pursuit of which belongs particularly to the Fellow-Craft stage.'

The division between scientific and occult astrology that I have outlined is confined to the higher branches of the art, and unknown to the casual reader of newspaper horoscopes.

Modern writers and astrology

Apart from fully committed astrologers, there have been many intellectuals who have shown an interest in the subject. Auguste Bouché-Leclerq, author of a massive treatise, *L'Astrologie Grecque*, made the remark that: 'One does not waste one's time

in studying how other people have wasted theirs.' This vie
was shared by many other scholars, Franz Cumont, Franz Bc
Carl von Bezold, Aby Warburg and Fritz Saxl, to name only
few. All these writers made their contributions to the study
astrology's place in history.

On the literary front the picture is even more interesting.
is not surprising that astrology, with its esoteric flavour,
elegant system of typology, and its echoes of magic ar
mythology, should appeal to many poets and novelists.

W. B. Yeats was one who had a strong penchant for tl
occult and was for a time, along with Aleister Crowley and
number of other well-known occultists, a member of a socie
called the Hermetic Order of the Golden Dawn. Some of h
poems show an interest in the symbolism of astrology. One, f
instance, entitled *The Poet Pleads with the Elemental Power*
begins:

'The Powers whose name and shape no living creature knov
Have pulled the immortal Rose;
And though the Seven Lights paused in their dance ar
     wept,
The Polar Dragon slept,
His heavy rings uncoiled from glimmering deep to deep:
When will he wake from sleep?'

Here the 'Seven Lights' are clearly the traditional seve
planets, while the 'Polar Dragon' is a concept in Hind
astrology.

Another writer fascinated by astrology was Frederick Rolf
alias Baron Corvo, that strange, brilliant, misanthropic, marty
like figure, the facts of whose unhappy life have been set out i
A. J. A. Symons's fascinating biography *The Quest for Corv*
Several passages in Rolfe's work testify to his interest i
astrology. One of them occurs in his remarkable novel *Hadria*
the Seventh in which Rolfe's own frustrated ecclesiastical amb
tions are fulfilled in fantasy by his hero, George Arthur Rose
who becomes Pope Hadrian VII. One passage in the boo
describes a conversation between Hadrian and a young theo
logical student whom he wishes to help. Finding the yout

eserved and uncommunicative, the Pope tries a different line
f questioning:

' "How old are you?"
"Twenty-nine."
"In which month were you born?"
"In July."
"In England?"
"In England." A rapid horoscopical calculation let
Hadrian know the lines on which to proceed.'

The youth's reply indicated that he was probably born in
Cancer, a sign for which Rolfe had a particular affection since
t was his own. He talks about the sign in another novel, *The
Desire and Pursuit of the Whole*, in which the central character,
Nicholas Crabbe, is Rolfe in thin disguise. This is how Rolfe
describes his aptly named hero:

'Under his shell, in fact, your crab is as soft as butter, and
just one labyrinthine mass of the most sensitive of nerves.
From which pleasing experiment [ie dissecting a crab] you
should learn to be as merciful as God to all poor sinners
born between the twenty-first of June and the twenty-fourth
of July: For they are born under the constellation Cancer;
and their nature is the nature of a crab. They are the clever-
est, tenderest, unhappiest, most dreadful of all men.

Clever men and dreadful men are not invariably unhappy:
but crab-men are all three—excepting on one sole condition.
That condition is their union with a Saturnian, born between the twentieth of December and the twenty-first of
January, who is their diametrical opposite and complement,
soft outside, hard within.'

One could hardly find a writer more different from Rolfe
than D. H. Lawrence, and one might be surprised to find astrology in his writings. Yet there is something very like it in
Lawrence's last book, *Apocalypse*, in which he calls for a return
to primitive man's union with the cosmos. At one point he
says:

'The sun, like a lion, loves the bright red blood of life, and can give it an infinite enrichment if we know how to receive it. But we don't. We have lost the sun . . .

And we have lost the moon, the cool, bright, ever-varying moon. It is she who would caress our nerves, smooth them with the silky hand of her glowing, soothe them into serenity again with her cool presence.

. . . there is an eternal vital correspondence between our blood and the sun: there is an eternal vital correspondence between our nerves and the moon.'

In another passage, Lawrence declares that:

'We and the cosmos are one. The cosmos is a vast living body, of which we are still parts. The sun is a great heart whose tremors run through our smallest veins. The moon is a great gleaming nerve-centre from which we quiver forever. Who knows what power Saturn has over us, or Venus? But it is a vital power, rippling exquisitely through us *all the time*. And if we deny Aldebaran, Aldebaran will pierce us with infinite dagger-thrusts. He who is not with me is against me!—that is a cosmic law.'

Coming nearer to the present day, we find that the writings of Henry Miller are full of astrological references. An anthology of these, compiled by Sidney Omarr, has been published in the United States under the title of *Henry Miller: His World of Urania*. In his foreword to this book, Miller says:

'Astrology does not offer an explanatio ws of the universe, nor why the universe exists. W to put it in simplest terms, is to show us that the rrespond-ence between macrocosm and microcosm. In short, that there is a rhythm to the universe, and that man's own life partakes of this rhythm. . . .'

In *The Colossus of Maroussi* there is a magnificent description, true to astrological tradition, of the sinister properties of Saturn:

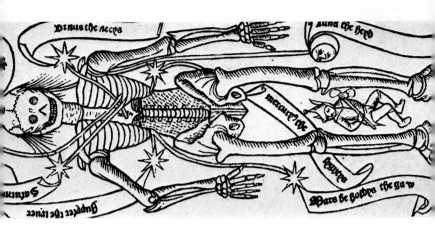

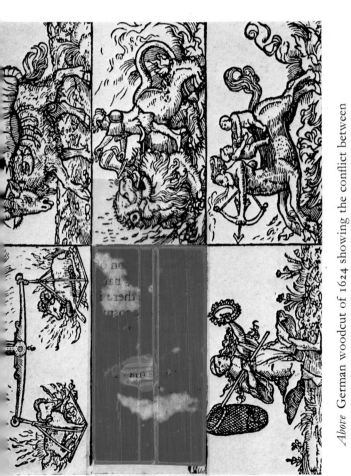

Above German woodcut of 1624 showing the conflict between opposing signs of the zodiac

Right Illustration of the relationship between the planets and the various organs of the body, from the *Calendar of Shepherds*, 1503

Frontispiece to the 1831 edition of Zadkiel's *Herald of Astrology*.

'Saturn . . . a living symbol of gloom, morbidity, disaster, fatality . . . arouses associations with tripe, dead gray matter, vulnerable organs hidden from sight, loathsome diseases, test-tubes, laboratory specimens, catarrh, rheum, ectoplasm, melancholy shades, morbid phenomena, incuba and succuba, war, sterility, anaemia. . . . Saturn is malefic through force of inertia. Its ring, which is only paperweight in thickness, according to the savants, is the wedding which signifies death or misfortune devoid of all significance.'

To the novelist's view of astrology it is interesting to compare that of certain mystically inclined philosophers like Gurdjieff and his pupil Ouspensky. The latter includes a section on astrological symbolism in his *A New Model of the Universe*. In another book, *In Search of the Miraculous*, he describes Gurdjieff's attitude towards the subject:

'We were walking in the park. There were five of us besides G. One of us asked him what his views on astrology were, whether there was anything of value in the more or less known theories of astrology.

"Yes," said G., "it depends upon how they are understood. They can be of value and they can be without value. Astrology deals only with one part of man, *with his type*, his essence—it does not deal with personality, with acquired qualities. If you understand this you understand what is of value in astrology." '

I

Introduction

At various periods in history astrology was used by its prac titioners in an attempt to direct natural forces and to contro their environment in various ways. Some used it for medica purposes, some for aiding military expeditions, some for find ing lost objects. The people who used astrolgy in these magica ways tended to combine it with other esoteric sciences— alchemy, palmistry, geomancy, and so on. Thus it was natura to regard these various systems as being linked in some way This view gained in popularity during the Renaissance thank to the revival of interest in Hermeticism and other orienta cults. Astrology came to be regarded as part of an ancien magical tradition, enshrined in which were secrets that enable the initiate to control natural phenomena in any way he pleased Although there may be some foundation for this belief, it ha lost much conviction because of the confused way it has bee expressed in the writings of occultists like Eliphas Levi an Aleister Crowley. Although the connection between, for in stance, the Tarot and astrology is a highly debatable matter, i has been argued over so often that I feel it should at least b discussed.

One man who did perhaps more than anyone else to popular

ise the magical tradition theory was the German, Cornelius Agrippa von Nettesheim (approx. 1486–1536). Agrippa was a strange figure about whom many bizarre legends grew up. He was supposed, for example, to have been accompanied everywhere by a familiar spirit in the form of a black dog called Monsieur. In his works astrology is linked with palmistry, alchemy, medicine, and almost every other science that one can think of.

Agrippa's theory of magic is set out in his *De Occulta Philosophia*, a work which contains little original thought but which summarises the whole of Renaissance magic. According to Agrippa the Universe is divided into three worlds, elemental, celestial and intellectual. The forces emanating from the creator are transmitted via the angels in the intellectual world and the stars in the celestial world, to the plants, animals, metals and human beings of the elemental world. The magician believes that he can draw down the forces of the higher world by operating in various ways on the lower.

Agrippa includes a section on celestial magic in which he discusses the making of images for attracting the celestial powers. The planets and the gods of the decans all have their special images. Saturn, for example, is 'a man with a stag's head, camel's feet, on a throne or on a dragon, with a sickle in the right hand, an arrow in the left'.[1] The Sun is 'a crowned king on a throne, a crow at his bosom, a globe under his feet, robed in yellow'.[2] Venus is 'a girl with loose hair wearing long white robes, holding in the right hand a branch of laurel or an apple or a bunch of flowers, in the left hand a comb'.[3] A talisman engraved with the Saturn image bestows long life. The Sun promotes success in all undertakings and protects the owner against fever. Venus gives strength and beauty.

The Cabala

The kind of magical theories that we find discussed by Agrippa and subsequent occultists owe a great deal to the Jewish tradi-

[1] Op cit., II, 38.
[2] Ibid, II, 41.
[3] Ibid, II, 42.

I*

tion that is enshrined in a series of documents known as the Cabala (I have adopted the simplest spelling in preference to the numerous alternatives, eg Kabbalah, Quabbala). Agrippa and his contemporaries liked to think that the Jews first learned their secret knowledge during their captivity in Egypt and that the Cabala was based on a tradition stretching far back into Egyptian history. This theory has now been discredited and it is thought that Cabalism, like Hermeticism, is of more recent origin. Nevertheless it does constitute a firm and influential tradition, and one in which astrology plays a not insignificant part.

The two most important extant books of the Cabala are the *Sepher Yetzirah* or Book of Formation, and the *Zohar* or Book of Splendour. When these were composed is not known exactly, but the former is thought to date from about AD 500, and the latter from rather more recently, probably about AD 900.

In both books the belief in celestial influence is evident. In the *Zohar* we read:

> 'Appointed over all these stars and constellations of the heavens are heads and leaders and ministers and it behoves them to give service to the world, each in accordance with his designated function. Nor does the smallest blade of grass in the earth fail to have its specially appointed star in heaven. And also, every star has a designated being over it, to represent it according to due rank, in ministrations before the Holy One, be blessed.
>
> Acting as guardians over this world are all the stars of the firmaments, with each individual object of the world having a specially designated star to care for it.'[1]

The *Zohar* also contains astrological references of a more veiled and symbolic nature. One chapter, for example, contains a description of the significance of numbers. In it occurs the following passage:

> 'The source is one and the current makes two. Then is formed a vast basin known as the sea, which is like a channel

[1] *Zohar*. Ed. G. G. Scholem.

dug into the earth, and it is filled by the waters issuing from the sea; and this sea is the third thing. This vast basin is divided up into seven channels, resembling that number of long tubes, and the waters go from the sea into the seven channels.'[1]

The 'source' mentioned in this passage is clearly the *Primum Mobile* and the seven channels are the emanations of the seven planets.

One of the cornerstones of the cabalistic system is the belief in the mystical significance of the letters in the Hebrew alphabet. According to the cabalists, the most powerful magical formula is that of the tetragrammaton which consists of the four letters JHVH which spell out the name of God. There is also a connection in cabalism between certain of the letters and the signs and planets. The seven double letters—Beth, Gimel, Daleth, Kaph, Pe, Resh and Tau—correspond to the planets, as we see from the following passage in the *Sepher Yetzirah*

'These seven double letters, he [God] formed, designed, created, and combined into the Stars of the Universe, the days of the week, the orifices of perception in man; and from them he made seven heavens, and seven planets, all from nothingness.'[2]

The chapter goes on to elaborate this relation and attributes a particular day, organ of perception, quality and planet to each letter. These correspondences can be summarised as follows:

Letter	Quality	Planet	Day of week	Organ of perception
Beth	wisdom	Moon	first	Right eye
Gimel	health	Mars	second	right ear
Daleth	fertility	Sun	third	right nostril
Kaph	life	Venus	fourth	left eye
Pe	power	Mercury	fifth	left ear
Resh	peace	Saturn	sixth	left nostril
Tau	beauty	Jupiter	seventh	mouth

[1] Ibid.

[2] *Sepher Yetzirah*. Tr. Wynn Westcott.

The following chapter of the *Sepher Yetzirah* deals with the relation between the signs of the zodiac and the twelve simple letters, He, Vau, Zain, Cheth, Teth, Yod, Lamed, Nun, Samech, Ayin, Tzaddi, Qoph. A passage in the *Sepher Yetzirah* refers to this relation as follows:

> 'These twelve letters he designed, formed, combined, weighed and changed, and created with them the twelve divisions of the heavens, the twelve months of the year, and the twelve important organs of the frame of man, namely the right and left hands, and right and left feet, two kidneys, the liver, the gall, the spleen, the intestines, the gullet and the stomach.'

According to another cabalistic document, the Book of *Arb 'at' al*, the firmament and the kingdom of heaven are divided into 196 provinces which are ruled over by seven supreme angels each of whom governs a particular planet and is endowed with his own special powers. The angel known as Hagith, for example, ruled over all matters connected with Venus and could transmute gold into copper and vice-versa. Another angel, Ophiel, ruled over matters relating to Mercury and could transmute quicksilver into white stone.

The cabalists believed that a knowledge of these basic relationships gave them a magical power of the physical world. By the use of a particular sign it was possible to invoke the force of a planet or its ruling angel and direct the resulting powers to material ends.

Another of the devices used by the cabalists and engraved on their amulets was the series of magic squares containing sets of interrelated numbers and corresponding to the various planets and metals. They called these squares *Kame'a* from which our cameo is derived. These squares are of ascending size, the smallest being the one corresponding to lead and Saturn which is set out as follows:

$$\begin{matrix} 4 & 9 & 2 \\ 3 & 5 & 7 \\ 8 & 1 & 6 \end{matrix}$$

Each vertical column and horizontal row in this square, as well as the two sets of three figures forming the diagonals, add up to fifteen which is the sum of the Hebrew letters forming the shortened version of the Tetragrammaton. The total of the nine numbers adds up to forty-five which is the sum of the full Tetragrammaton. When used as an amulet this was engraved on a sheet of lead.

Jupiter, Mars, the Sun, Venus, Mercury and the Moon all had respectively larger squares whose numbers were related in a similar way.[1]

Many volumes have been written about the symbolism in the Cabala and I cannot in a single section do more than scratch the surface of this extremely complicated subject. My purpose is merely to show the close connection between cabalism and astrology.

Alchemy

Although alchemy and astrology go hand in hand through the history of medieval and post-medieval occultism the origins of the two sciences do not coincide. Whereas the beginnings of astrology can be pinpointed, those of alchemy are a matter for speculation. Some historians hold that it originated in China, while others believe it to be of ancient Egyptian origin.

The latter theory is encouraged by and to some extent based on, the frequent use of the word 'Hermetic' in connection with alchemy. Much alchemical literature is supposed to be based on the revelations of Hermes Trismegistos, the mythical Graeco-Egyptian figure whom I discussed in Chapter 2. An enormous number of works were attributed to Hermes even though many of them bore no relation to the original Hermetic texts. Thus the word 'Hermetic' came to be used extremely loosely of anything vaguely connected with alchemy.

One of these documents was the so-called 'Emerald Table of Hermes' which became the bedside creed of the medieval

[1] A full account of the magic squares and the correspondences set out in the Book of Arb 'at' al is found in *Amulets and Superstitions* by Sir E. A. Wallis Budge.

alchemists. The name derived from a legend that the thirteen precepts of the creed had been found engraved on an emerald slab discovered in the tomb of Hermes by Alexander the Great. In order to show its astrological colouring I shall quote the table in full.[1] It reads as follows:

'1. I speak not fictitious things, but that which is certain and true.

2. What is below is like that which is above, and what is above is like that which is below, to accomplish the miracles of one thing.

3. And as all things were produced by the one word of the Being, so all things were produced from this one thing by adaptation.

4. Its father is the sun, its mother the moon; the wind carries it in its belly, its nurse is the earth.

5. It is the father of perfection throughout the world.

6. The power is vigorous if it be changed into earth.

7. Separate the earth from the fire, the subtle from the gross, acting prudently and with judgement.

8. Ascend with the greatest sagacity from the earth to heaven and then again descend to the earth, and unite together the powers of the things superior and the things inferior. Thus you will obtain the glory of the whole world, and obscurity will fly away from you.

9. This has more fortitude than fortitude itself; because it conquers every subtle thing and can penetrate every solid.

10. Thus was the world formed.

11. Hence proceed wonders which are here established.

12. Therefore I am called Hermes Trismegistos, having three parts of the philosophy of the whole world.

13. That which I had to say concerning the operation of the sun is completed.'

Though alchemy may not have originated in Egypt it certainly flourished there, especially in the period of Greek domination. Later it was taken up by the Islamic world and

[1] I quote this table from the version given in *Prelude to Chemistry* by John Read.

further developed there. A theory which the Arabs conceived was that all metals and minerals were formed by the interaction of two basic substances, sulphur and mercury. When Islamic learning began to penetrate Christian Europe in the twelfth century, alchemy as well as astrology came with it.

In the hands of the medieval scholars alchemy was further elaborated. The sulphur-mercury theory was modified by the addition of a third element, salt. These three substances were given a symbolic meaning. Mercury corresponded to man's spirit, sulphur to his soul, and salt to his body—a theory that is often represented by a triangle in alchemical symbolism.

Rodney Collin in his *Theory of Celestial Influence* says that the three elements were also associated with the three forces represented by the Sun, the Earth and the planets. By changing the order of these three, he says, it is possible to arrive at six different permutations which are the basis of six cosmic processes and six alchemical operations. The latter are known as coagulation, dissolution, sublimation, putrefaction, separation and transmutation.

The basic connection between astrology and alchemy is the correspondence between the seven planets and the seven alchemical metals. The two superior metals, gold and silver, were associated with the Sun and Moon respectively; while the five planets corresponded to the five metals as follows:

Mercury	mercury
Venus	copper
Mars	iron
Jupiter	tin
Saturn	lead

These correspondences, known as 'affinities', were not applied solely to the effort to manufacture gold. They also became the basis of a highly complex system of physiology. Man, it was held, contained within him different quantities of all metals and therefore had affinities with all the planets through different parts of his body. A man who had one part of his body highly developed was thought to have a special affinity for the corresponding planet.

Astrology has survived and flourished where its sister science, alchemy, has long since faded. It is not impossible, however, that the latter will one day be revived.

The Tarot

The pack of cards known as the Tarot has for many centuries been a favourite method of fortune-telling, particularly among the gipsies. It has also exercised an enormous fascination over many writers. To quote only one example, T. S. Eliot had the Tarot in mind when he wrote, in *The Waste Land*, of Madame Sosostris the famous clairvoyante with her 'wicked pack of cards'.

The Tarot consists of seventy-eight cards which are divided into 'minor arcana' and 'major arcana' or trumps. The minor arcana are fifty-six in number and are divided into four suits, wands or sceptres, cups, swords, and pentacles or money. Each of these suits contains fourteen cards—four court cards and ten number cards. The major arcana consist of twenty-two cards numbered from 0 to 21, each card bearing a different symbolic picture, eg the Juggler, the Emperor, Death, the Moon, the Hanged Man, the Chariot.

In spite of its enormous influence the origins of the pack are shrouded in mystery and the precise meanings of the symbols on the cards remain obscure. There are those who believe the pack to be a forgery, concocted in the late fourteenth century by the astrologer and cabalist Jacques Gringonneur to amuse King Charles VI of France. Other theories place its origin in India and China. But, to quote one authority, MacGregor Mathers:

'the great exponents of the Tarot, Court de Gebelin, Levi and Etteila, have always assigned to the Tarot a Quabalistico-Egyptian origin, and this I have found confirmed in my own researches into the subject, which have extended over several years.'

It is impossible, in this section, to set out all the different theories on the origin of the Tarot pack; but it is worth remarking that several authorities on the cards have made out convincing cases for their relation to the Cabala and to astrology.

It seems extremely likely that there is a correspondence between the Cabala and the Tarot. The fact that there are twenty-two letters in the Hebrew alphabet and twenty-two trumps or major arcana in the Tarot would otherwise be a remarkable coincidence. If we accept this correspondence, then we must also accept the astrological significance of the cards, since, as we have seen, the *Sepher Yetzirah* clearly sets out the relation between the signs and planets on the one hand and the Hebrew letters on the other. There remains, however, the problem that three of the letters, Aleph, Mem and Shin (known as the three 'mother letters'), are unaccounted for in astrology. Papus, in his thorough but controversial study, *The Tarot of the Bohemians*, states simply that these three letters have no astrological affinity. He favours instead the theory that the seven planets each act in three different ways, thus producing twenty-one different emanations corresponding to twenty-one of the major arcana (that is, excluding the Foolish Man which is numbered zero).[1] Another authority, Oswald Wirth, claims that the twenty-two trumps correspond to twenty-two constellations, some of which are signs of the zodiac, others not.

Papus also has an interesting theory on the relation between the signs of the zodiac and the four suits of the minor arcana, wands, cups, swords and pentacles. The three fire signs correspond, he says, to wands, the three air signs to swords, the three earth signs to cups, and the three water signs to pentacles.[2]

There are countless more theories on the meaning of the Tarot, all of them speculative. It is not my purpose to add to these speculations, but merely to show that the theory of a correspondence between the Tarot and the symbolism of astrology has been widely supported.

[1] Op. cit., Ch. 16.
[2] Ibid, Ch. 17.

Chapter 11   How the horoscope works

The outlines of calculation

The average person's knowledge of astrological theory comes from his contact with the subject through popular newspaper astrology. If the reader of a daily newspaper looks at the entry for his zodiacal Sun-sign in the horoscope column, he will find a short paragraph containing a number of non-committal and highly general statements and pieces of advice. He will be told to 'avoid risks', 'seize opportunities', or possibly 'take advantage of financial openings'.

If the reader were anxious for more detailed advice than this he would have to seek a private consultation with an astrologer. If he did so he would probably be offered a number of different services, for instance, a general character analysis, a forecast for the next few years or a forecast about a particular event. What process would the astrologer go through in order to provide this information?

The procedure of casting a horoscope must always start with certain pieces of information, namely the date, place and preferably time of birth. How this is translated into a horoscope varies from country to country and from astrologer to astrologer. To simplify matters I shall outline only one system—one that is commonly used in Britain.

The object of the calculations is to construct a 'map' of the heavens at the time of birth showing the relative positions of the planets, signs, and houses. To do this, the astrologer is armed with an ephemeris, that is a table of planetary positions for the year in question, and a table of houses, containing

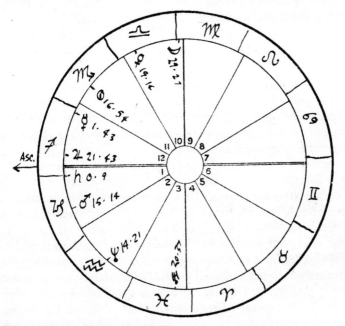

The horoscope of King Edward VII

entries for different parts of the globe and showing where the ascendant and mid-heaven would fall at a given time of day.

The astrologer's blank chart, before he begins his calculations, consists of a circle divided into twelve segments. His first step is to find out the native's ascendant, that is the sign that was over the eastern horizon at the time of birth. In the case of the sample chart shown above, the rising sign was Sagittarius and the ascendant lay at 27 degrees 37 minutes. Having determined this, the astrologer, using the equal house system, is able to enter the other signs, placing the cusps at thirty-degree intervals around the outside of the circle. Next, he turns to the ephemeris and enters the Sun, Moon and each of the planets in sign and house. In this case the Sun is 16 degrees 54 minutes in Scorpio. The layman would take this to mean that the native was 'a Scorpio', but the cognoscenti regard the Sun-sign as only one of many factors and one which does not necessarily determine the person's 'type'.

The elements of interpretation

From these hieroglyphics the astrologer must now deduce what sort of person the native is, what the main strengths and weaknesses in his personality are, and what the main trends of his life will be. If he wishes to make precise predictions about the future the astrologer can do one or both of two things. First, he can cast a 'progressed horoscope' in which the positions of the planets are symbolically projected into the future, using each day after the person's birth to represent a year in his life. Secondly, he can examine the 'transits' for any given day, that is to say the actual positions of the planets vis-à-vis those of the natal chart and, if he wishes, those of the progressed chart.

Whatever kind of horoscope he is casting, the astrologer's interpretations will be based on the traditional meanings of the signs, planets, and houses. He will also have to take into account the aspects of the planets, that is to say the angles formed between one planet and another, some of which are regarded as harmful, and others as beneficial. In the next few pages I shall attempt to outline the traditional meanings given to the various elements in the horoscope.

The planets

Sun ☉

From the astrologer's point of view the Sun is the most important of the heavenly bodies. It represents the general motive and vitalising force of the native's character. It is also an indication of his personality, that is the face that he presents to the world. The native's zodiacal 'type' is frequently determined by the Sun's position in the zodiac. A strong ascendant can, however, be equally significant. Traditionally the Sun is a benefic *advantage* and its influence is considered almost invariably good, though it can, if badly placed, lead to bombast and ostentation. *trouble*

Moon ☽

Whereas the Sun stands for the outward personality, the Moon represents the sensitive inner nature. The Sun is active and masculine, the Moon passive and feminine. The qualities it imparts are timidity, affection, receptiveness, impressionability, moodiness, and a liking for the seclusion of a home environment. The so-called lunar type is depicted as being 'moon-faced', with a placid, dreamy disposition.

Mercury ☿

This planet takes its name from a Roman god who was, in turn, a translation of the Greek god Hermes, the nimble, light-footed messenger, the god of travel and commerce. Accordingly the planet is believed to impart quickness of wit and talkativeness. It is traditionally neither a 'benefic' nor a 'malefic', but one that can take on either quality depending on its position. In the *Tetrabiblos*, Ptolemy writes that when Mercury is in a good position it renders the mind 'prudent, clever, capable of great learning, inventive, expert, logical'. But when badly placed 'he makes men busy in all things, precipitate, forgetful, impetuous, frivolous . . . and altogether of slippery intellect, and predisposed to error'. The planet gives us our word 'mercurial', meaning capricious.

Venus ♀

Originally associated with the goddess Ishtar of the Babylonians, Venus has always been associated with motherhood and hence with love and the sexual act. Traditionally it is a benefic. According to Ptolemy:

'When Venus rules alone in a position of glory, she renders the mind benignant, good, voluptuous, copious in wit, pure, gay, fond of dancing, abhorring wickedness . . . but, if contrarily posited, she renders the mind dull, amorous, effeminate, timorous, indiscriminating, sordid, faulty, obscure and ignominious.'

Mars ♂

In Babylonian times Mars was associated with the warlike god, Nergal. The Roman god whose name the planet bears was also the god of war. Hence the planet imparts belligerent, aggressive qualities. Although traditionally a malefic, Mars is now thought to be beneficial if well placed. To quote Ptolemy again: 'Mars alone having dominion over the mind, and placed with glory, makes men noble, imperious, irascible, warlike, versatile, daring, bold . . . but posited ingloriously, he makes men cruel mischievous, sanguinary, tumultuous, extravagant in expense, boisterous, ruffian-like, precipitate, drunken, rapacious . . .'

Jupiter ♃

Traditionally Jupiter is a benefic and even the Gnostics regarded its influence as good as my earlier quotation from the *Pistis Sophia* shows. Jupiter is now associated, like Mercury, with intellectual activity. But whereas Mercury is the quick, sprightly, witty dabbler, Jupiter is the profound, far-reaching thinker. In modern terms, Mercury is the journalist, Jupiter the philosopher. The planet is also associated with generosity, affability and friendliness. Hence our word 'jovial'.

Saturn ♄

In ancient and medieval times Saturn was the most feared of all the planets. Its influence was thought to be almost entirely baneful, governing old age, sickness, death, imprisonment, and imparting dourness, coldness and inhibition. In the second *Astronomicon* of Manilius there is the following passage describing Saturn:

'Where the world sinks at the foundations of heaven and lost in midnight beholds above it the opposed sky—that is the region where Saturn exercises his strength. Of old was he himself cast down from the Empire of heaven and the seat of the gods. . . . A dread title belongs to his realm: *Daemonium* the Greek hath it: and the name betokens clearly the power that dwells here.'

Today the attitude towards Saturn has changed somewhat. Although it is still regarded as being restrictive and inhibiting, these qualities are thought to be desirable in certain circumstances.

Uranus ♅

The discovery of Uranus by Sir William Herschel in 1781 was the first discovery of its kind for several thousand years. It upset the old seven-planet theory and posed a problem for the astrologers. They soon incorporated it into the system, however, and attributed to it qualities of violent change, revolution, and sudden awakening. It bestows an urge for freedom, and an original, versatile mind.

Neptune ♆

Discovered in 1848, Neptune also has no traditional associations. Modern astrology, however, has allotted to it qualities of deception, nebulousness and subtlety. In his textbook *The Principles of Astrology* Charles E. O. Carter says of Neptune: 'It commonly produces extreme sensitiveness, physical and emotional, and is not only prominent in the nativities of musicians, but also mediumistic persons.'

Pluto ♇

Discovered in 1930, Pluto does not yet seem to have taken on any very positive identity. Astrologers do not seem to be very clear about what its properties are. There is a feeling, however, that Pluto represents the sudden eruption of long-pent-up forces. In her *Modern Text Book of Astrology* Margaret Hone says: 'From the time of its discovery, much has gone on which is eruptive. That which was in the dark or bound or enclosed is violently ejected or vice-versa. One instance is the development of the atom bomb.'

The signs of the zodiac

The signs can be categorised in various ways. First there is the Fire-Earth-Air-Water division, each element ruling three signs. The qualities associated with the elements are roughly as follows:

Fire	volatile, forceful, restless
Earth	dependable, static, practical
Air	lively, unpredictable, communicative
Water	emotional, sensitive, unstable

The Fire and Air signs are said to be 'positive' and have an affinity for one another, as do the 'negative' groups, Earth and Water.

The other main division is into Cardinal, Fixed and Mutable signs. These categories encompass the following qualities:

Cardinal	dominating, outgoing, active
Fixed	cautious, conservative, steadfast
Mutable	adaptable, versatile, changeable

Now for a brief description of the characteristics of each of the signs.

Aries ♈   Fire, positive, Cardinal; ruler, Mars.

Although Manilius describes Aries as 'a gentle sign, open to the harm that falls on gentleness, free of guile, and with heart as soft as fleece that wraps his body', the sign is usually regarded in quite a different light. Isabelle Pagan in her study of the zodiacal signs, *From Pioneer to Poet*, describes Aries as follows: 'The type of fight congenial to the true Arietian is the "Forward charge!" He is the Captain, the Leader, the Pioneer among men. . . . Enterprise and ardour are the characteristics of the type.' This is much nearer to the accepted view of Aries as an aggressive, fierce-tempered, wilful sign. A typical Arien was Bismark, born with his Sun in Aries; another was General Gordon, born with Aries rising.

APR 20-MAY 20

Taurus ♉ Earth, negative, Fixed; ruler, Venus.

The sign of Taurus comes under the Earth element and the typical Taurean is, accordingly, a down-to-earth, practical sort of person. The Venus rulership makes the Taurean loving, affectionate and kind. Normally he is placid and even-tempered, but can be as terrifying as a bull on the rare occasions when he is roused to anger. The ruler, Venus, gives the Taurean a loving disposition and a strong sexual instinct. The stolid Oliver Cromwell was born with his Sun in Taurus. Less typically Taurean was Adolf Hitler, born with his Sun near the cusp between Aries and Taurus.

May 21 – June 21

Gemini ♊ Air, positive, Mutable; ruler, Mercury.

The main characteristics of Gemini are self-expression, eloquence, intellectual energy, and versatility. Mercury is the planet of the mind and Gemini represents Mercury in his capacity as an artist and agile manipulator of ideas. The versatility of Gemini can become a fault by diffusing the Geminian's energies over too wide a range of activities. Also the Geminian can often be vacillating and indecisive. John F. Kennedy, in his ability as a speaker, in his intellectual agility, and in his reliance on intellectual qualities, was in many ways typical of Gemini, his Sun-sign.

June 22 – July 23

Cancer ♋ Water, negative, Cardinal; ruler, Moon.

Frederick Rolfe's description of the crab's attributes that I quoted in the last chapter exactly sums up the main Cancerian qualities—outwardly hard and unemotional, but inwardly sensitive in the extreme, not only to other people, but also to art,

literature, and psychic forces. Another prominent characteristic of the Cancerian is his clannishness and preference for his
family and home environment. Rolfe was one type of Cancerian;
Madame Blavatsky, with Cancer rising, was another, demon-
strating the psychic qualities of the sign. The Cancerian is
essentially an emotional, feeling type, rather than a thinking
type.

July 24 - Aug 23

Leo ♌ Fire, positive, Fixed; ruler, Sun.

Unlike the devious and difficult Cancerian, the Leonian is
straightforward, uncomplicated and outgoing. The Sun rulership gives him a strong, attractive personality and makes it
easy for him to command loyalty from others. These qualities
make him a natural leader, and the sign has long been associated with kings and potentates. The faults that sometimes
afflict the Leonian are vanity, pomposity and greed for power.
Mussolini, who had his Sun in Leo, had many good Leonian
qualities, but in the end succumbed to the faults of the sign.

Aug 24 - Sept 30

Virgo ♍ Earth, negative, Mutable; ruler, Mercury.

Like Gemini, Virgo is ruled by Mercury and is mental in
character. But the Virgoan tends to apply his mental talents to
more practical activities than does the Geminian. Virgoans are
down-to-earth, methodical, conscientious, and skilful with
their hands. They are fond of things to do with the country and
the soil. They are aloof by nature and do not as a rule make
many friends. Lyndon Johnson, with his reserved, withdrawn
temperament, his predilection for the practical, and his love
for his ranch, is typical of Virgo, his Sun-sign.

Sepr 24 - Oct 23

Libra ♎ Air, positive, Cardinal; ruler, Venus.

This is one of the most easy-going and gentle of the signs. The
scales symbolise a love of harmony and balance and a distrust
of unpleasantness and conflict of any kind. Unlike the Virgoan,
the Libran is sociable and outgoing, and generally makes many
friends. Like the Taurean, who is also ruled by Venus, the

Libran is fond of the opposite sex. His balanced outlook and dislike of extremes make him a good diplomat, but they can also lead to weakness and an inability to commit himself. Gandhi's devotion to peace and non-violence were typical of his Sun-sign, Libra.

Scorpio ♏ Oct. 24 – Nov 22 Water, negative, ~~Fixed~~; rulers, Mars ~~and Pluto~~.

Scorpio has all the energy and forcefulness of Mars, combined with the emotional intensity associated with its watery nature. The Scorpionic type is extreme in his feelings towards others, sensitive to injury, quick to anger. He is ambitious and dislikes playing second fiddle. He can be vindictive, and cruel. More than any other sign, Scorpio is associated with sexual energy. Writers as different as Manilius and Alberuni agree in attributing rulership of the genitals to Scorpio. Martin Luther, whose Sun-sign was Scorpio, had the Scorpionic qualities of leadership, sensitivity, and volatile temperament. These same qualities were manifested differently in Napoleon Bonaparte, who had Scorpio rising.

Sagittarius ♐ Nov 23 – Dec 21 Fire, positive, ~~Mutable~~; ruler, Jupiter.

This sign has the Jupiterian qualities of strong intellect tending to express itself in more profound, philosophical ways than in the case of Gemini. Sagittarians are noted for their love of sport and outdoor life. They are restless, generous, adventurous, exuberant and fond of travel. The fault of the sign is a tendency to become boisterous and vulgarly jovial. Winston Churchill was born with his Sun in Sagittarius, and had the sign's qualities of strong intellect and thrusting determination. The same qualities were shown in Cecil Rhodes and Theodore Roosevelt, born with Sagittarius rising.

Capricorn ♑ Dec 22 – Jan 20 Earth, negative, ~~Cardinal~~; ruler, Saturn.

Capricorn, ruled by the dour old man, Saturn is unemotional, solemn, and lacking in humour. The adjective 'saturnine' aptly sums up the qualities of the sign. At the same time, the Capri-

K

cornian is tough, determined and practical. Although he moves slowly, he is very difficult to stop once he has set his mind on a goal. He is a good organiser and has the ability to withstand and overcome hardships. The latter quality was outstanding in the Emperor Augustus whose Sun-sign was Capricorn, as he proudly proclaimed. The solemn, steadfast Gladstone also displayed many qualities of Capricorn, his rising sign.

Jan. 21 - Feb. 18

Aquarius ♒ Air, positive, Fixed; rulers, Saturn and Uranus.

The water-bearer shows some of the characteristics of Saturn, being serious and undemonstrative in emotion. But the sign also takes on some of the qualities of its other ruler, Uranus. Whereas the Capricornian is a respecter of tradition, the Aquarian is the reverse—revolutionary, unconventional and individual in his thought. He does not make close friendships, for his feeling is for humanity as a whole and often leads to altruistic activities. Charles Dickens, whose Sun-sign was Aquarius, had both the humanitarianism and the intellect of the sign. John Ruskin, born with Aquarius rising, was also typical of the sign with his far-ranging ideals and his schemes for the betterment of mankind.

Feb 19 - marzo

Pisces ♓ Water, negative, Mutable; rulers, Jupiter and Neptune.

The Piscean has the Jupiterean intellect, but is negative in personality, reacting to situations and people rather than imposing himself on them. He has the Neptunian qualities of sensitivity and nervousness and tends to live in a world of dreams and imagination. Hence many Pisceans are poets, novelists and artists. The composer, Chopin, whose Sun-sign was Pisces, is a good example. The Piscean is a lively and entertaining companion, but is inclined to be moody.

The Houses

As I explained in Chapter 2, the houses are twelve imaginary divisions of the earth's surface projected into the sky. Each sign, therefore, moves into a new house roughly every two hours. The cusp of the first house, known as the ascendant, is thought to be a very important indicator of the native's character. Each of the other houses has its association with a different area of everyday life. The following table is a rough indicator of these associations.

1st	house	personality, physical appearance, childhood
2nd	house	possessions, money
3rd	house	family relations, communication, speech
4th	house	parents, childhood home, seclusion
5th	house	the native's children, sexual act, creativity
6th	house	the native's subordinates, work, health
7th	house	marriage, partnership, close friends
8th	house	death, accidents, mysticism
9th	house	study, mental exploration, travel
10th	house	career, ambitions, attainments
11th	house	ideals, worthy causes, societies
12th	house	restriction, sorrow, illness

Interpretation of the specimen chart

The birth-chart shown on page 123 is that of King Edward VII. I shall not give a full interpretation of it, but merely point out some of the important features in order to give an idea of how an astrologer approaches a chart.

This horoscope has a number of outstanding features. First of all the sign of Sagittarius is, for several reasons, remarkably strong: first, because it is in the ascendant; secondly, because its own ruler, Jupiter, is present in the sign; thirdly, because Mercury is also in the sign. Here is a clear case of the ascendant being stronger than the Sun-sign which, in this instance, is Scorpio. The Sagittarian qualities were unusually pronounced in Edward. He was generous, exuberant and jovial. And, as might be expected, his joviality tended at times to vulgarity. The Sun in Scorpio made him sensitive beneath his boisterous exterior, strong-willed, emotional, aggressive, and passionate in love. His amorous side was strengthened by the fact that Venus is in her own sign, Libra.

Another remarkable thing about the chart is that the planet nearest to the ascendant, Saturn, is in its own sign of Capricorn, giving a strong Saturnian flavour to the nativity. The combination of Saturn and Capricorn in the first house suggests a hard and difficult childhood. Edward was indeed subjected to a rigidly disciplined upbringing.

Both of the two strongest planets, Saturn and Jupiter, are square in aspect (ie at ninety degrees) to the Moon. The square aspect indicates difficulty and conflict, and the Moon often represents the person of the mother. In this case there is a strong indication that the native had a thoroughly inharmonious relationship with his mother—which, in the case of Edward, was true.

On the whole it is a strong chart, and one suitable for a king.

Having surveyed the history of astrology and seen how it has defied the sceptics and survived into the present day, it is now natural to ask: how meaningful is the science that astrologers profess? I should like to try to answer this by dividing my enquiry into three separate questions: first, how valid is the astrological tradition as it stands? Secondly, is there any scientific evidence that, even in the most general way, the heavenly bodies influence life on earth? Thirdly, in the light of the answers to the first two questions, is there any future for an astrological science of any description?

First, the astrological tradition. How valid is the complex system of rules whose progress we have traced from Babylonian times to the present day? There are two possible grounds on which this case can be argued: a scientific ground, and an empirical one. People arguing for and against astrology often tend to confuse the two and thus add to the woolly cloud which surrounds most debates on the subject. In order to clarify the argument it is necessary to examine the two cases separately.

First, the scientific. I can say right away that there is no scientific defence to be made for the astrological tradition. (I repeat, the *tradition* as it stands. I am not talking about *any* astrology.) Why do I say this? My main reasons are as follows.

The lynch-pin of the whole traditional astrological system is the zodiac. In early Babylonian astrology, as we have seen, the zodiacal signs represented actual groups of stars along the ecliptic, and the tradition, as it later developed, was based on the powers believed to reside in these constellations. Now, as I explained in an earlier chapter, the precession of the equinoxes has caused the signs of the zodiac to move out of alignment with the constellations with which they were originally associated. The inference from this is clear: either the astrological tradition became obsolete as soon as the precession began to affect the alignment of signs and constellations, or else the qualities attributed to the signs are not connected with the stars at all.

Another important concept in astrological theory is that of the planetary aspects. These are based wholly on geometrical patterns formed on a sheet of paper, and are not related in any way to modifications of the planetary forces brought about by changes in relative position. Furthermore, the traditional astrologer, when calculating the planetary positions, makes no allowance for the velocity of light. Thus in the case of Saturn, for example, whose light can take as much as an hour and a half to reach the earth, the apparent position of the planet at any given time would be many degrees different from its actual position.

There are other arguments, but these two should be enough to show that the astrological tradition cannot be defended on scientific grounds. This does not mean that it cannot be defended on other grounds. In answer to the objections that I have raised to the tradition, the astrologer might reply:

> 'What you say is true, but astrology is not based on a causal relationship between man and the planets; therefore, to disprove such a causal basis is not to disprove astrology—in fact your remarks are irrelevant. Astrology is simply a system of symbolism which has been found to express profound truths about human beings.'

This is a fair point, and it leads us to examine the empirical case for the tradition. There is no doubt that such a case exists.

I shall try to bring forward some of the most convincing pieces of evidence.

One of the men who investigated astrology on an empirical basis was the psychologist Carl Jung whose most important findings on the subject are set out in a short book called *The Interpretation of Nature and the Psyche*. Jung chose astrology as the subject of an experiment designed to test a theory he had developed about a principle that he called 'synchronicity'. He had for some time believed that certain events—such as exceptional runs in gambling, predictive dreams, and other 'meaningful coincidences'—pointed to the existence of a mysterious law that was not chance and yet was not causal. This was what he termed 'synchronicity'.

Jung believed that synchronicity was essentially a psychic principle. He described it as follows:

'Synchronicity . . . consists of two factors: (a) An unconscious image comes into consciousness either directly (ie literally) or indirectly (symbolised or suggested) in the form of a dream, idea, or premonition; (b) An objective situation coincides with this content. The one is as puzzling as the other.'

How was Jung to put his finger on this elusive principle? Looking for a method of testing it by statistical analysis, he decided that astrology provided the best subject. He set out to examine the horoscopes of a number of married couples to see whether they bore out the traditional astrological features associated with marriage, namely either the conjunction of one partner's Sun with the other's Moon, or the conjunction of the two moons.

Jung analysed altogether the horoscopes of 400 married couples. His investigations yielded some interesting results. The frequency of the two marriage conjunctions among the horoscopes analysed was not high enough to indicate that the results were anything more than chance. But equally important from Jung's point of view was the fact that the two aspects mentioned came *first in the order of frequency of all the aspects noted*.

This result proved Jung's point. If the occurrence of the two marriage aspects had been higher than chance would allow, then it would have seemed likely that a causal principle was at work. Instead what had occurred could only qualify as a coincidence, but clearly a meaningful coincidence, as was proved by the grouping of the aspects relative to one another. In short, the result qualified perfectly as a synchronistic phenomenon.

Another researcher in this field is Dr Hans Bender of the Institute for Border Areas of Psychology at Freiburg. In 1952–4, Bender carried out an experiment with the help of 150 astrologers. The experiment consisted of two types of test. First, the astrologers were asked to try to determine the life histories of a number of people by studying their horoscopes, after which their calculated life histories and the real ones were compared. Secondly, the astrologers were asked to make blind character analyses from the horoscopes. The results of the first test were unimpressive, but in the second test several astrologers made amazingly accurate diagnoses.

From the evidence so far, we can draw the following conclusions: (a) traditional astrology can be effective in certain cases; (b) the effectiveness of the system is not based on scientifically verifiable causal laws; (c) instead, a psychic principle seems to be involved.

What is this psychic principle and how does it work? It is not possible to describe it, but only to point to certain examples of its occurrence. In the *Interpretation of Nature and the Psyche*, Jung mentions the experiments of Dr. Rhine, who discovered that certain subjects were able to read 'telepathically' the numbers on a series of cards and perform other feats of extra-sensory perception with a greater degree of success than chance would allow.

'We must ask how it was,' Jung says, 'that Rhine succeeded in obtaining positive results. I maintain that he would never have got the results he did if he had carried out his experiments with a single subject, or only a few. He needed a constant revival of interest, an emotion with its characteristic *abaissement mental*, which tips the scales in favour of the unconscious.'

In other words, the subject needs to believe in a system of divination if the system is to work. Furthermore all systems of divination work, up to a point, if they are entered into in a spirit of strong belief. Astrology is easier to believe in, at any rate for the modern mind, than other systems of divination. We think in causal terms and therefore it is easier for us to accept a system which appears to have a causal basis than one which does not.

We have seen how astrology has what Jung calls a synchronistic basis. Next we must ask if there is a causal element as well —which brings us to the second of our three main questions. Leaving aside the astrological tradition, we must now ask: Is there any scientific evidence that the heavenly bodies influence life on earth in any way? The answer is yes, and there is a great deal of evidence to support this.

The *Observer* of 1st October 1967 carried a report by the paper's science correspondent, John Davy, on the recent discovery of a wind of gas blowing out from the Sun at a speed of about 1 million mph and consisting mainly of ionised hydrogen which is extremely sensitive to magnetic and electrical influences.

Furthermore the Earth is surrounded by an invisible magnetic ocean known as the 'magentosphere'. The Sun has a similar magnetic ocean, and the solar wind carries with it a magnetic force deriving from this ocean. At the point where the Sun's magnetic field meets that of the Earth, disturbances occur which are believed to have far-reaching consequences, affecting for example the weather on earth.

Even more interesting is the belief that these solar emanations are influenced by the Moon and planets. The report mentions a leading Australian physicist, Dr. E. G. Bowen, who claims that magnetic storms are more frequent when Venus or Mercury is at inferior conjunction, that is to say is lined up between the Earth and the Sun.

Moreover, these solar disturbances are believed to be related to certain kinds of mental illness. To quote the report: 'Three doctors in Syracuse, New York State, have found that magnetic storms coincide with increased admissions of mentally disturbed patients to two local mental hospitals. The effect is slight but statistically significant.

'As a working hypothesis, the doctors have been wondering if magnetic disturbances can upset mental function through interference with electrical processes in the brain, and have been experimenting with volunteers exposed to fluctuating magnetic fields. They found some changes in ability to perform various simple tasks. The whole matter is still obscure, but suggestive.'

Some very interesting findings have emerged from the researches of Michel Gauquelin, a member of the staff of the French *Centre National de Recherche Scientifique*, who has been investigating the claims of astrology ever since he studied psychology and statistics at the Sorbonne. Having read the works of Paul Choisnard and the *Traité d'Astrobiologie* of Karl Ernst Krafft, he decided that their work was unsatisfactory from a scientific point of view. He therefore decided to conduct his own statistical investigation, and in due course examined 50,000 horoscopes.

Although, unlike Jung, he was unable to find any evidence to support traditional astrology, he nevertheless discovered, somewhat against his will, some puzzling facts. In examining the horoscopes of 25,000 distinguished professional men from all over Europe, he discovered an abnormally high incidence of the prominence in the charts of certain planets, namely the Moon, Mars, Jupiter and Saturn. Furthermore he found that the prominence of any one of these planets tended to be connected with a particular profession or group of professions. This is how Gauquelin described it in his book *L'Astrologie devant la Science*:

'In each country the same results appeared. Although separated by frontiers, customs, different languages, the new-born chose to come into the world under the same planet when, later in life, they were to choose the same vocation, whether they were Frenchmen, Italians, or Germans. However absurd this may seem, a more and more precise relationship manifested itself between the moment of birth and the professional destiny of certain distinguished men.'

One of Gauquelin's findings was that most people born with Mars rising or at the mid-heaven tended to become doctors, sportsmen or army officers. On the other hand, actors and members of Parliament preferred Jupiter.

Gauquelin rejected, absolutely, any explanation based on astrological theories. Instead he developed what he called his theory of 'planetary heredity', based on the idea that children tend to be born under the same cosmic conditions as their parents. To prove this theory he made fifteen hundred comparisons of parental and child horoscopes and found that there was a significant similarity between them. There also emerged some interesting ancillary facts; for example, the resemblance between the child's chart and that of the parents was more marked when the two parental charts were similar. Gauquelin's explanation is that at the moment of birth certain planetary forces come into effect, accelerating or decelerating labour. The effect, he claims, works through the planets that are nearest to the earth, namely the Moon, Venus, Mars, Jupiter and Saturn.

The researches that I have mentioned all indicate, albeit in very general terms, that the heavenly bodies do have some sort of influence over human life.

We now come to the third and final of the three questions posed at the beginning of this chapter: in the light of the findings we have discussed, what, if any, is the future for astrology?

The researches that I have discussed show that the planetary movements can be an indication of human characteristics. A child born in September with Venus in conjunction with the Sun will, other things being equal, be different from one born in May with Venus and the Sun in opposition. But how different? And in what respects different? Science has not yet provided us with the sort of intricately detailed answers that traditional astrology provides. Yet conceivably science will one day be able to provide this detail.

In one sense it is not necessary for traditional astrology to readjust itself to the discoveries of science, for, as I have pointed out, the old system will always work provided that the person practising it is able to approach it in the right frame of mind and has the right sort of intuition. But how much more powerful will his intuition become if he knows that the symbols he is working with are not just conventions, but represent real forces. If astrology is able to revise itself completely in the light of science, then it will benefit immensely and greatly increase its already impressive following in the world.

Index